THE

Writing Lives of Children

Dan Madigan
Victoria T. Koivu-Rybicki

Stenhouse Publishers
York, Maine

Stenhouse Publishers, 431 York Street, York, Maine 03909

Library of Congress Cataloging-in-Publication Data

Madigan, Dan.
    The writing lives of children / Dan Madigan and Victoria T.
Koivu-Rybicki.
      p. cm.
    Includes bibliographical references (p.   ).
    ISBN 1-57110-011-3 (alk. paper)
    1. Storytelling—United States. 2. Children—United States—
Diaries. 3. Language arts (Elementary)—United States. I. Koivu-
Rybicki, Victoria T. II. Title.
LB1042.M24 1997
372.67'7—dc21   96-51055
                                        CIP

Cover and interior design by Darci Mehall, Aureo Design
Cover illustration by Chauncy Brown, Jamar Stuart, and Darryl Thrash
Typeset by Achorn Graphics

Manufactured in the United States of America on acid-free paper
01 00 99 98 97 9 8 7 6 5 4 3 2 1

For Paul
and all of our children
Vicki

For Pat, Toby, Tom
Dan

and for the children whose voices we
represent in this book

Contents

Acknowledgments

We are thankful for those who have worked with us over the last five years to develop a dynamic language arts classroom where learners were the focus of attention. We are especially grateful to those who contributed an extensive amount of time in the classroom as guest teachers: to Bill for his insightfulness regarding literacy issues and his original ideas that contributed to the initial development of the Writers' Community; to Sylvia, Jackie, Tegan, Connie, and Lisa for their countless hours of volunteer teaching in the classroom and community service to the children and their parents; to all of the other visitors who volunteered and contributed extensively to our curriculum; to all of the community members, including the school and district administration, who have supported the literacy learning of our students and who have supported our risk taking as teachers. Thanks to all who have encouraged our students to achieve and who have supported us every step of the way as we have pursued this collaborative teaching endeavor. Above all, we thank our courageous young authors, who have dared to reveal themselves as writers and who have taught us the multiple ways in which writing contributes to living and learning.

Introduction

Dan Madigan exited the expressway and turned onto the familiar four-lane street that took him to Franklin Elementary School. The business corridor hadn't changed much during the years he had been traveling the northwest route through the city: morning rush-hour traffic, high school kids waiting for city buses, a railroad crossing, stoplights strategically placed overlooking busy intersections. As he turned right and drove down Newcombe Street, he noticed the familiar blue milk crate attached a third of the way up a telephone pole, a makeshift basketball hoop built by nine-year-old Allen, one of the neighborhood children. Behind the pole, on the other side of a cyclone fence, was the Franklin Elementary School complex, a city block containing a playground and a two-story brick school building. Across the street from the school on all sides were postwar-vintage homes, separated from the school complex in the front by a two-lane street and in the rear by a one-lane potholed alley. Dan drove slowly down Newcombe. Groups of neighborhood children were approaching the school from different directions. Eight- and

1

ten-year-olds walked in small groups, while younger children held the hand of an older brother or sister. The front of the school served as a gathering point for backpack-laden children, and the steps of the school as a strategic place for last-minute exercise.

Dan entered the alley behind the school and squeezed his Subaru in between the dumpster and Vicki Koivu-Rybicki's car. He thought back to the first time he and Bill, a colleague, had visited Franklin as guests of Vicki, an inspiring language arts teacher at the school and a graduate school classmate of his. Vicki and Mr. Jarrid, the principal, met them just inside the door. Mr. Jarrid, pleasant but serious, asked, "So why are you here at Franklin Elementary? We have not had good experiences with university people who have come to *study* us. They leave and we have gained nothing. What I want to know is how are you going to help our children as learners?"

000

The physical spaces of the school and the neighborhood haven't changed much, and Mr. Jarrid's questions are as important today as they were then. This glimpse of the educational environment in which we have taught together for the past five years is intended to create a space from which other stories can emerge. It has not described the changes that have taken place since we began our collaboration in 1989. What has changed is that visiting teachers—like Bill, Connie, Tegan, Lisa, Jackie, and Sylvia (each of whom has spent a significant amount of time in Vicki's classroom as a co-teacher over the past five years)—have moved on to other teaching initiatives involving children. What has also changed is the way Vicki's students see themselves: they now know that they too are authors and teachers who share knowledge with others. As for ourselves, we have grown as educators in our understanding of the complex issues that affect children's language learning.

This is a book about storytellers and their stories. Our students are the storytellers. Their written poems, essays, and short narratives serve as vehicles for stories about their complex lives. When Jermaine wrote a poem about his impulsive reaction to the sight and smell of his mother's cheeseburger, he also created a space for a good story to emerge. Patterned

2

after "This Is Just to Say," a poem by William Carlos Williams, his poem went like this:

I'M SORRY!

Look at mommy's cheeseburger sitting on
    the table.
While I'm sitting in the living room
    watching cable.
Watching channel 41 as you can see.
Look at the cheeseburger attrackting to me.
I picked it up and there's nothing to it.
I ate it . . . I guess the devil made me do it.
So mommy please forgive me!
     I'm sorry!
      I'm sorry!
       I'm sorry!

We all remember vividly Jermaine's class presentation of his poem. Reading between the lines and the concrete images of the poem, his classmates heard an emotion-packed oral description of his mischievous act. He was sorry, yes, but he was also rather proud of his cunning and industry.

As classroom members, we too are storytellers whose narratives affect what Jermaine and the other children fondly call "The Writers' Community." Vicki has taught at Franklin for seven years and in the city for thirty; Dan taught language arts for fourteen years in a rural high school. For several years, as a graduate student and then as an assistant professor of English, he commuted eighty miles from his university to Franklin every week to work with Vicki. Often, in preparation for class, whether before school, during lunch, or after school, we find an empty classroom and share stories about children whose actions have impressed us. At other times, distant only from the physical environment of the school, we write stories about our teaching experiences as a way to understand the subtle nuances that influence our lives as teachers. After a hectic and frustrating Sunday morning spent thinking about schoolwork, for example, Vicki wrote this in her personal journal:

There is so much to do that I have a hard time starting. I am overwhelmed. So after church and Bible studies classes for the children . . .

3

I came home, prepared dinner, and went to bed for two hours. I hate sleeping during the day . . . When I awoke I came upstairs to do some school work. I looked over all the papers the children had done this week. It took hours . . .

For each of us, these stories relieve some of the familiar frustration that results from teaching, if only for a moment. Together, however, our individual stories about children provide us with a more comprehensive narrative about ourselves as teachers and about our students and their storied lives, which deepens our understanding. What follows is an example of one of our stories, which develops out of a series of e-mail conversations between us. Vicki first began writing about Taria in the fall of 1992.

Taria is a child [third grade] who signs-writes everyday. She writes stories and brings them to school . . . She writes like Diane, a similar style. She has no idea of the use of a period. She has signed to communicate with her hearing impaired mother since she was one . . . Language is her life. She takes on many of the responsibilities in the home. She told me last week she won't get toys for Christmas any more. She will receive books and clothes . . . I introduced her to the class . . .

Since 1992, we have written dozens of similar focused narratives about Taria. When woven together, they form a rich description of a child not only as a literacy learner but as a human being directly influenced by the social, political, and historical structures that affect the communities in which she lives.

For our students and for ourselves as teachers and researchers, we turn to story as the preferred way of telling others, outside our classroom, about our experiences together in a writing workshop environment. We recall eight-and-a-half-year-old Amani's guarded response to a request from a visiting preservice teacher. "Tell me about your experiences as a writer."

Amani stiffened and nervously slid down in her chair.

Our visitor tried again, but this time she directed her words to the child sitting next to Amani. "From all the stories you have written, which one is your favorite?"

Suddenly, Amani sat up and spoke, "The alley behind my house was scareeee. At night, when I'm looking out my window I see . . ."

Amani did not respond directly to the visitor's request. Instead, she told a story. As we have come to expect, this is typical of Amani. When Amani shares information about her life, she does so within the framework of a story. It's her way.

As writers and teachers of writers, we relate closely to Amani's learning experience as an interpreter of her world. When we first started teaching together, we were asked to present our experiences with our students and their writing at a conference. We agreed, but found ourselves struggling over our presentation. How could we represent the children in ways that would reveal their complexity as feeling, thinking, imaginative individuals? How could we present them in ways that would not patronize or objectify them? How could we involve them in the conference? We didn't need to search far for an answer. As we stood back from our work, we recognized that we consistently relied on our own narratives about the children, specifically their own stories, as an important way of knowing about them as writers and readers. Consequently, for the presentation we created a narrative in which we layered the multiple voices and experiences of children and prepared a dramatic reading to frame the narrative.

At first, our audience seemed caught off guard, but soon they warmed to Vicki. She began by describing Cathy, a nine-year-old child from our Writers' Community. Midway through the story, Vicki's voice took on an urgent tone:

> Cathy's energy surged. Firmly she gripped a sharpened pencil and methodically punched at a blank piece of lined paper. Quick blows to the paper in rapid succession. Faster and faster.

As her voice trailed off, Dan's voice emerged, describing a scene at the back of Vicki's classroom:

> Four children sat in their desks, tightly packed. The front of the desks touched and dared to overlap, just as the children's stories touched and overlapped. Jacob, one of the occupants of the desks, held several children spellbound as he detailed his inventiveness and fearlessness in rescuing his parents from a burning building. "It is truuuue," he pleaded convincingly.

Although there are many ways of framing and interpreting the complex relationships in which our students engage every day as writers and readers of their world, for us, story has become the familiar, reliable way. Having said that, we want to emphasize that writing is by no means the only form of expression capable of capturing the essence of a story. In fact, as we and our children realize now more than ever, writing is often a limited way of telling a rich story. Only a couple of miles from the Franklin school is one of the artist Diego Rivera's most famous frescoes. Our students have visited the fresco, and they are fascinated by the stories of human experience Rivera tells through this montage of image and color and form. As the students examined the details of the fresco, they talked about their own working-class heritage. In doing so, they began to understand the culture that Rivera spent his life expressing through his art.

For our children, drawing, dancing, painting, and making music are preferred methods of expression. After Kevin read Toshi Maruki's *Hiroshima No Pika*, for example, he struggled to articulate his feelings about the children and adults who were left homeless after the dropping of the atomic bomb. His written journal entries were sparse. Kevin considered his drawing much more representative of the event and of his feelings about it. Many of our children turn to alternative forms of expression to make concrete the abstract in their lives. Aniece represents much of her life through music. The same is true for Shalice, who claps, stomps, and hums to musical notes and melodies that she arranges in her head. "I want to be a singer and tell others about my feelings," she says.

Our purpose in writing this book is not to duplicate available titles about children's use of multiple forms of expression in their language development. Art and drawing in the language arts classroom have already been carefully described by such authors as Ann Alejandro ("Like Happy Dreams—Interpreting Visual Arts, Writing and Reading"), Steve Moline (*I See What You Mean*); Anne Dyson ("Appreciate the Drawing and Dictating of Young Children"), and Ruth Hubbard (*A Workshop of the Possible*). Instead, we draw on their work in order to understand how children use multiple forms of self-expression to communicate. In a dynamic language arts environment children use music, art, writing, and reading in overlapping ways to understand their lives and improve their skills as communicators. Our purpose is not to reinvent the writer's and reader's workshop, which we heartily embrace. Many books already describe the writing workshop in detail, for example, *Writing: Teachers and Children at Work*, by Donald Graves; *Living Between the Lines*, by Lucy Calkins; and *When Writers Read*, by Jane Hansen.

Several decades ago, writer Harold Rosen wrote that stories were being devalued in our culture, that the art of storytelling was dying. At the same time, communities were becoming fragmented in ways that deemphasized storytelling as a way of understanding. Today, in a world of sound bites, we might readily agree with Rosen's observation. But that would be a hasty mistake. From our perspective, storytelling is indeed alive and well. Artists, psychologists, historians, anthropologists, novelists,

The falamys
are being sprite

feels for the
little girl.

2-8-94 Hiroshima No Pika
Toshi Maruki
The book sad becuse
the little girl cloley
loasing her mother
Father. this how it fily's
lik haveing a bome
2-9-94 rite behind you I can
put my sif in this book
because the little girl is in
her home and boom a bome
2-10-94 in-your nice city
I have font out
that thare was mor
people then the peopl
2-11-94 in that city, When the little
2-11-94 gile was in the eickbder
a I had filyng for sher.

Kevin describes a Hiroshima family devastated and separated by the bomb.

teachers, and students, to name a few of those concerned with human events and experiences, rely on stories. This book is a modest attempt to represent and reinforce this view.

For the most part, the narrative style we have adopted allows us to distinguish the overlapping and competing narratives children employ to represent their reality. We see the young writer as a person operating in a particular context in which cultural meanings are already deeply embedded. A child's choices as a writer—topic, subject, format, words, and audience—are influenced by the child's relationships to other members of that community. As writers, children are also shapers of their own culture and of their individual and collaborative roles within that culture. We hope to shed light not only on how a child comes to write about a particular idea, and for whom, but also on how a child is affected by what she writes and who, in turn, is affected by her writing.

We have chosen to write about ten children from among the many who were members of our Writers' Community. We have done so, however, with caution. Whenever we are asked to represent the children we teach, we first ask ourselves a question: How can we represent the true complexity of any one child and his or her actions as a literacy learner? To say representation is possible, or possible only through writing, is to risk claiming too much. What we have come to terms with is that writing, like other forms of expression, is one part of a larger whole. When we work with student writers, we ask them to record their ideas and experiences in language that is clear to them and to their readers. We also remind them to be true to their own experience in their stories, poems, plays, and essays and sensitive to those people and issues they write about. We extend this truth and sensitivity to our own writing (we have changed students' names as well as the name of the school and of the community in which they live).

Our self-imposed demand for truthfulness has been difficult at best. One book about ten children cannot begin to represent the writing culture of all the students in our classroom over the past five years. And even though we have worked painstakingly to remain true to the voices of individual children, our representation encompasses only a small part of the variety of overlapping cultures within which the children live and learn. We have attempted to capture the essence of each child as a complex individual engaged in the complex act of writing. As teachers, and as parents of children of our own, we feel that this is important. While the topics children choose to write about in their daily lives may appear similar, the situations they remember and describe are always particular. We believe that in order to understand another person, we must seek to particularize that individual.

As teachers of writers, we understand the writing process to mean much more than "X" number drafts of any written piece. Any written artifact involves diverse, often competing narratives that represent the reality of the writing process. Our own narratives, as well as those of other students, parents, and community members, influenced individual children to write as they did. Our stories in the following chapters seek to describe this process. We have, of course, left out some important voices, but like any tellers of human experience, we made choices that were often influenced by the limitations of writing and of our own literary style. In the end we have recorded the short writing journeys of ten unique children in the hope that readers will begin to understand children as writers and that they will use the stories we tell to generate and explore new ideas about children and literacy learning.

One final note. Although each child's story has its own particular meaning in relation to literacy learning, each story is also connected to a larger story. We invite readers to skip around and consider connections. Readers might also want to sample the conclusion first, interviews we conducted with each other that address issues not explicitly touched on in the text. (Vicki's role as an experienced teacher in an inner-city environment, for example, is not directly addressed in any of the children's stories, nor is assessment of student learning.) But however readers choose to read this book, we hope that they will encounter children from a perspective not celebrated often enough by those of us who write about children.

Latoya: Public Stories About Private Lives

Mrs. Bedford was a tall, lean woman who usually wore long, simple cotton skirts and blouses. The outfits seldom matched and the colors were often washed out or faded. She usually wore shoes that appeared ill-fitting and uncomfortable. Her hair was tied back and she wore small gold loop earrings. On most days, I noticed her entering the building near 9:30 A.M. to report for her duties as a lunchroom mother, an infant and toddler in tow. She struggled with the rickety makeshift stroller over the large rug at the front entrance to the school. The crying baby was bundled in blankets and the little girl held on to her mom's skirt. No other lunchroom mothers brought their children to school. No other mother was willing to share so much about herself and her family at the time.

Vicki's description of Mrs. Bedford serves as a reminder of how the private lives of our students and their families converge in the public setting of school. Sometimes these lives are revealed in subtle ways. For example, Mrs. Bedford's actions around the school, her attention to children in tow while carrying out hall duties, revealed her pride as a care-giver, and the fact that she couldn't afford day care for her children or a ride to work. At other times, individual students and their families are more overt about sharing their personal lives. Mrs. Bedford, for instance, eventually approached Vicki and asked her for assistance in learning to read more fluently. She explained that because of her lack of education she was a poor reader, but she wanted to learn better so she could help her young daughter become a better reader. She also wanted to prepare for her G.E.D. (high school equivalency diploma).

When our students and their families share their lives with us, we learn a great deal and come to rely on such sharing to inform our teaching. Our experience with Mrs. Bedford is a case in point. Because she was willing to talk about her family and herself, she and Vicki established a better relationship, one that proved invaluable later, when her daughter entered our fourth-grade classroom.

〓〓〓

A new school year.

Students in motion. Erupting. Sliding in and out of desks. Struggling for control of the pencil sharpener. Whimsically discussing their lives. Thirty-six new and gangly nine- and ten-year-old children. Faces without names. Such were the first few days of our new school year. But as always happens in our classes, after the first week names begin to stand out.

Latoya Bedford. Mrs. Bedford's daughter. She was a shy but competent reader, and she liked the challenge of writing. For extended periods of time during the first few weeks of the school year, she wrote, a serious activity for her. Her first completed story, only several sentences long, was noteworthy:

In one class we write . . . We make story. I walk to school. How can I get there on time?

11

It was a good beginning for a new writer, but little did we know its full complexity until we began to file the students' stories for the week. On the back of Latoya's story two sentences dangled at the top of the page.

Why do people kill if? If people stop killing, maybe the world would be a better place.

We paused in our filing. Latoya, nine years old, was already trying to take an active role in solving problems that were extremely difficult even for adults.

As it turned out, Latoya's first story foreshadowed her particular reason for writing: to share with other readers her private thoughts about her life and her community. Latoya was worried about getting to school on time because, like most of the other children who attend our neighborhood school, she walked. But Latoya's story also reveals a deeper layer. Many of our children, including Latoya, assume responsibility for taking care of their siblings. They often come from large families. Their parents and guardians, employed as factory and service workers, are subject to difficult working conditions and schedules, odd shifts, frequent job changes, and long hours. As a consequence, the older children in the family assume responsibility for their younger siblings. Each morning, Latoya made sure that her two younger sisters ate a good breakfast and dressed warmly. Then she escorted them to school, to their lockers, and to the kindergarten and first-grade classrooms. We understood why Latoya was worried about getting to school on time.

However, domestic duties were not all that concerned her. She wanted to stop the violence and the killing. This hope is not unusual among the children we teach. Many of our students are concerned about the daily violence that permeates their lives. They often hear gunfire from the surrounding neighborhood.

One pleasant fall day, as we walked with our students around the neighborhood, Alissa proudly pointed to her house on the corner across from the school. Then, in a low voice, she told us she often lay in bed at night, scared, because of the gunfire she heard outside. Violence is a fact of life for the children in our school. And even if they are sheltered from it while at school and in their homes, they encounter daily reminders of the violence in their city on television and in other media. These children are often at a loss in trying to figure out how they might intervene to change a violent world. What is their role? Are they responsible in any way?

As we read Latoya's brief story, we wondered what questions were on her mind. We were drawn to the seriousness of the subject matter. She was one of the first students that year to use writing to express her fears about violence. It seemed that she saw the violence around her as a personal matter, something she wanted to confront in the more public forum of her shared writing.

As the year progressed, Latoya continued to negotiate the three concerns—writing, family, and violence—she first wrote about in September. She used writing as a framework for exploring the convergence of her family community with the larger community. She wrote about growing up and being a doctor so she could help others as she once did her sick sister. She wrote about her early life in an apartment with cousins, and a family trip to Mississippi—good times, as seen through the eyes of an appreciative narrator. Through November, Latoya was comfortable sharing her personal thoughts about life in her family. In late fall, however, a change occurred. Vicki's December 1 letter to Dan captured the moment:

> Latoya told me she had a problem with her writing. She gets ideas but sometimes doesn't write them down completely. When she shares her reflection journal entry, she puts her journal down and tells the rest. I told her that I sometimes want to explain my writings further and that we both needed to practice writing down what we think. Maybe we hesitate because it doesn't sound as good as the way someone else writes. Maybe our reading, practicing, and listening to others' writings could help us find better ways of expressing ourselves.

Over the years, we have noticed that any number of different things can affect children's writing. Writer's block, we have found, is not age specific. Our response is to give encouragement to students who are stuck. We ask them to reflect on the possible cause of their writing problems. We try to motivate them to push beyond it. We are not sure which of Vicki's suggestions Latoya followed, but within a couple of weeks she submitted the most complex of the stories she wrote that year. It was a story that merged the themes of family and violence, and the private and public worlds of a young child. It was a story about her uncle, a recent victim of a violent robbery. Later conversations with Latoya suggest that "My

Uncle" had been on her mind for a long time, but it was a story not easily told or shared with others.

> My Uncle was killed. Why was he killed? I would like to know. I heard that it was because he would not give a man a dollar . . . I think my uncle was killed for no reason. When I think of him I just want to cry.

After reading Latoya's story, we began to understand what might have caused her writing problem. Her "ideas" were personal and tragic. No wonder she couldn't write easily and fluently, as she had about her trip south. And once she had decided to write about her uncle, Latoya needed time to sort things out—to weigh the value of committing her experience to paper, where others could read it. Latoya apparently knew, from previous experiences of sharing her writing with other children in her class, that once she made her story more public, she might be forced to think about even more complex questions. After reading "My Uncle," Mary wrote in the margins: "Did you write this because it was bothering you? If you did, how did you feel when you had thoughts about him?"

Such questions are revealing. Writing and telling stories can be cathartic. And yet negotiating meaning through writing is not complete just because a story has been written down and shared with others. In fact, it might just begin when a story has been written down. Such a thought was reflected in a more direct question from another child who also reviewed "My Uncle." James wrote, "Why did you write about your uncle?"

We believe that Latoya intuitively knew her story might have an impact on others; by writing "My Uncle" and sharing it, she took advantage of the process and was able to grow remarkably as a writer. She thoughtfully considered the questions her friends had asked her about her story and made a concerted effort to answer them over time.

In what is a very mature strategy for a nine-year-old, Latoya went on to examine what it meant to be a writer. Her favorite author was Mildred D. Taylor, a writer who lucidly captures the essence of the black struggle and portrays women as problem solvers in a complex and often unfair world. For Latoya, Taylor understood what it meant to try to make sense of life through writing, and Latoya turned to her for assistance in answering the tough questions about why authors write. Within several days of sharing "My Uncle" with the class, Latoya wrote in her Reflection Journal:

14

2/12 Dear Mildred D. Taylor,

I wish I was a writer like you. You write great books. Are all of your books something that happened in your life?

Your friend,
Latoya

2/13 Dear Mildred,

Roll of Thunder is a great book. It shows you how to show your feelings. It must take you days or months to write a great book. What would you say to a young author?

Your friend,
Latoya.

Latoya's letters are interesting. She wrote them as a way to challenge her own thoughts about writing, but from our vantage point her questions are rhetorical. Latoya knew, from discussions in class, that authors often write about their lives and their feelings. We also suspect that Latoya might have written to Taylor as a way to imagine how a published writer might respond to an inquiring young author: *Listen to your own voice and don't be afraid of what you might discover as you write.* Latoya's journal letters to Taylor, along with questions her friends had asked her regarding "My Uncle," made one thing apparent to her as the year wore on: she discovered that writing might be a means by which to explore complicated ideas about the world.

If we ever doubted that this is what was on Latoya's mind, that doubt was erased in early April. As snow and sleet pinged on the windowpanes, distracting several students, Dan asked, "Are there any volunteers to read your newest story or poem?"

Latoya's hand waved tentatively. All eyes shifted toward her. In the background, there were serious murmurings. Several children prodded her to be even bolder. We knew their motive. Latoya had recently introduced her controversial story, "My Cousin," to a small group of her friends. They were overwhelmed with emotion and adamant that she share the story with the rest of the class. We had heard the rumbling in Latoya's group a few days before and had sat in on one of the discussions. "My Cousin" was indeed an explosive story, yet it was the kind of story that was ready to be told in our classroom, and a story that Latoya needed to tell.

On that morning, Latoya read her story to a group of attentive, awe-struck children and two wide-eyed teachers.

MY COUSIN

My special cousin's name is Dion. He shot himself in the head playing Russian Roulette. I found out about the death Easter night on the ten o'clock news. I was very very sad that my cousin is dead. I felt very bad because I never said to him, "I love you," in any way. His sister didn't get a chance to say it either because they were always fighting.

Dion and my uncle Jerry were downstairs playing on Easter morning. Dion told Jerry, "I'm going to play Russian Roulette." Then Jeff said, "Give me that gun." By that time Dion had pulled the trigger. All of that happened in my Uncle Paul's house while he was getting ready for bed.

Dion died on the way to the children's hospital. The funeral is Friday. I have one thing to say.

I Love You Dion

After interviewing Latoya about her story, we realized that it reflected her growth as a writer. She had become accustomed to writing as a way of sorting through her private feelings and ideas. She commented, "I wrote 'My Cousin' because I couldn't tell nobody my feelings. If I wrote it down, it wouldn't hurt as much as talking . . . They wouldn't look at his things. They closed his room up, and put all his things away . . . I was watching TV and somebody said that when someone in your family dies don't hide his stuff. It's better to talk about him than to hold all the feelings in. When something happens to the family it affects the whole family, it's better to write about it instead of trying to explain it."

Latoya's comments reveal how deeply she yearned for some kind of disclosure about the tragic events that led to the death of her cousin, yet, nothing was immediately forthcoming. No one in her family was talking. There was so much confusion: How did it happen? How could it have happened? For Latoya, understanding the tragedy meant confronting the issue head on, and writing appeared to be one of the few alternatives she had. Such a notion reinforced what she had already learned about writing and its possibilities. In writing about her uncle, she felt much better. Disclosure meant the beginning of a constructive dialogue with her peers about a senseless death.

Latoya commented, "The more I was by myself, the more I got confused, and I had to talk with people . . . I talked to a lot of my aunts and uncles and they were saying that it took a strong person to write something like this . . . They [family] told me that this story had encouraged other people [family members] to write about things that happened . . . I wrote it to get my feelings out, and keep my family closer together, and to let people know that we love each other."

Latoya's comments reveal her growing recognition of some of the possible purposes for writing, but they also alerted us to Latoya's emerging awareness that writing can have an effect on a more public world. Latoya had experienced the consequences of making public the personal matter of her uncle's murder. At that time, the students empathized with her and rallied behind her in condemning the violent behavior of an unknown suspect. But Latoya was less sure about the support she might receive over her cousin's possible suicidal death. Suicide is still taboo in our society, and the families of suicide victims often suffer as a result.

As Latoya remembered, "My first reaction was if I write it, it's going to be a bunch of problems. I'm going to have lots of people talking about my cousin . . ." Perhaps she also remembered how some students had teased her on one or two previous occasions. Before her classmates really knew her, they talked about her sagging socks, her worn clothes, and her "nappy" hair. In Latoya's mind, those taunts reflected upon her family as well. But despite her fears, Latoya pushed for comments about her new story. The results surprised her.

"Instead of them teasing me, they helped me a lot," said Latoya. "They said, I know how you feel . . . And, the more I talked to people [children], discussion came out about them and their families. It made me feel good that I helped others, and we helped each other as one."

One student, who was intensely interested in "My Cousin," reinforced Latoya's ideas about what we would call the "generative nature" of story. On the back of the copy of "My Cousin" Mary received as one of the editors of the class magazine, she wrote,

Latoya, I feel sorry that your best cousin died. You know how I feel because my best cousin died. It really hurts inside that you lost someone special in your heart. I did not have to read all of your story to know how you feel about Dion Branford.

Mary's reaction to Latoya's story represented the general reaction of the majority of the students in our class. They understood death as a loss, and Latoya's story captured this experience of loss in a meaningful way.

We often have the privilege of teaching the same group of students in both their third- and fourth-grade years, but mostly we lose track of our writers as they disperse during their final year of elementary school. Fortunately, we were able to interrupt that trend following Latoya's promotion to fifth grade. We worked out a program with two fifth-grade teachers that allowed eight to ten fifth graders to work once or twice a week with our third- and fourth-grade students. The following fall, Latoya, as one of the new mentors, picked up right where she left off the spring before.

As a fifth grader working with younger children, Latoya became an advocate for writing about life's experiences. She wrote and modeled such stories for herself and her students. "Talking wasn't enough," insisted Latoya to a group of writers. "Instead, express your feelings on paper, and that's better . . ."

She told new and younger writers, "The more I write it down there's more to think."

What Latoya meant was that writing served as a permanent reminder, a tangible product. "It's going to be there and you always keep it," she said.

As a result of her writing philosophy, other fifth-grade peer teachers referred troubled students to Latoya. Somehow those fifth graders sensed that Latoya's philosophy would be meaningful to particular third- and fourth-grade writers. "Latoya is the one to work with the kids who have a hard time. She can take their problems and turn them around," said Shalanda. In essence, Latoya told reluctant writers of her experiences with a lot of family members and friends who were troubled, and she told them that writing about one's experiences is helpful.

Marlowe was one of those reluctant writers. He was rebellious, obstinate, and convinced that he couldn't read or write. For him, and for everyone around him, writing time was problematic. Latoya stepped in. Each time the peer teachers met with the fourth graders, Latoya worked with Marlowe and several of his friends. In describing one of her meetings with Marlowe, she commented that Marlowe didn't like to do the writing work that the others were doing at the time. Consequently, she took him away from the class, into the corridor, and asked him to write what he could on paper. She supported him and encouraged him to write about what he knew or, more precisely, what was troubling him.

Latoya was a definite hit and influenced many of the young writers she worked with that fall. They felt comfortable in sharing more personal aspects of their lives. In fact, they came to look forward to such sharing. So, it came as a bit of a surprise to us in December when Latoya seemed to reverse her opinion about the value of writers sharing their private thoughts with others. In an e-mail note to Dan, Vicki wrote,

> Latoya has asked that we not publish "My Cousin" because she and her mom decided that it is too personal. The "personal" aspect became an issue when Latoya challenged Yvonne's "Neighborhood Story."

Latoya's apparent change of direction caused us to step back. She was not being consistent. Earlier, her mother had supported her decision to share publicly the story about her cousin. What was it about Yvonne's story that had influenced her to think about pulling it out of circulation? For answers, we looked back on the occasion when Yvonne shared her story with the class. In her journal, Vicki had written,

> Yvonne read her story to the class. She spoke of her neighborhood and how disgraceful it is. There is too much drug traffic, and no one dares walk to the park at night. The streets have broken bottles and there is noise of guns and loud music. Yvonne says that her friend's mom is a hooker and they were "shocked" to see her on the bed. She ends the story asking how are hookers happy with that life. [Dan, what did Yvonne and her friend see on the bed? The mother on drugs? Shooting up? Naked? With a man? I was happy that no one asked. The ending question by Yvonne left us all thinking.]

At the time, neither Vicki nor Dan could have guessed how Yvonne's story would influence the thinking of the children in the class. Then came Latoya's request to pull her own story from circulation and her intense challenge to Yvonne over the propriety of sharing her story: What if someone discovers the name of the woman? And what if someone gets the wrong idea about our neighborhood? Yvonne stood fast. She wanted others to read her story. She wanted change, and that could not happen, she said, unless others knew about the problem. From our point of view, Latoya had established a precedent. Her writing had profoundly influenced Yvonne, and in the long run, the precedent was not lost on Latoya either. By the time Yvonne's story was ready for publication in late December, Latoya's challenges to Yvonne had diminished and her support was more evident.

Events later that winter helped us understand that Latoya's actions could be attributed to her continued interest in the question of responsibility in sharing private thoughts in a public forum. If Latoya rejected her earlier beliefs during the year she was a peer teacher, it was only briefly. By January, she was again challenging reluctant writers to capture their feelings in writing. She encouraged Candler to write about his painful experiences in foster care, and she challenged Taria to think deeply about her experiences with a hearing-impaired mother. Finally, Latoya requested that "My Cousin," along with "My Uncle," be considered for an anthology that would showcase student writing.

Our experience with Latoya and her family has been enlightening. In sharing their personal lives with us and our students, they helped to initiate a constructive dialogue in which we all learned something important. We learned that Mrs. Bedford and her daughter were willing to risk the loss of some privacy to bring about constructive change in their lives. Mrs. Bedford eventually did go on to get her G.E.D., and her openness with Vicki enabled us to pursue further discussion about her family as it concerned her daughter. From Latoya we learned that when children write about events that are important to them, that are complex, that need to be unraveled and confronted, they have a greater sense of control over those events. Finally, we learned that when the world seems most confusing to children, we need to give them an opportunity to work through that confusion. We need to allow them to express the fears and the perceptions that most concern them. We need to give them something to hold on to. Writing a story about your own life provides such an opportunity. Latoya reminds us, "It's going to be there and you always keep it."

Jakeem; Living and Learning Through Writing

Hi, my name is Jakeem. I like to read and write, but mainly read. My readings help me with my writing a lot. My teacher is Mrs. Rybicki. She started me writing stories. But I always like to read. Now when I read I write after I read to give me an idea for something for me to make a story of. But ideas weren't always as easy to come by . . . I think "Emergency" got most of the attention. But my favorite writing was "Beauty." When I wrote the poem "The Gulf War was upon us" it made Mrs. Rybicki feel very happy because everyone else was writing bad things about the war. "Beauty" made a big difference in my whole class. They loved that poem. "Beauty" kept our minds off the War. To Mrs. Rybicki our writing is worth as much as gold.

Nine-year-old Jakeem finished reading his autobiography and with quiet hesitation scanned his audience—college writing students and prospective language arts teachers from a nearby university who were visiting our classroom. Intuitively, Jakeem asked for questions, which he fielded expertly. Finally, he invited his audience to meet with him during a breakout session, where he enthusiastically presented his poem "Beauty" and, as an aside, his story "Emergency." Both pieces were selections from his writing portfolio. Jakeem was a huge hit with the college students. Of course, we knew he would be. He is not only a likable child, he is also an engaging speaker. As teachers, we have learned to depend on Jakeem's inspirational support. When he was our student for two years, and a "teacher" for one year, Jakeem seldom failed to arouse an audience with his passion and optimism for life. From the first day Jakeem participated in class discussions, he seemed mature and confident beyond his years.

As we observed him closely over time, however, we discovered a child who presented himself to others as confident, but who was just beginning to build a feeling of confidence within himself. Jakeem's contrasting writings, "Beauty" and "Emergency," represent two sides of someone for whom confidence has not always come so easily.

His mother portrayed Jakeem as a shy boy. "He practiced looking mean so he could protect himself." He longed to be like his twin brother—aggressive, sociable, and talkative. Jakeem forced himself to play with other children in the neighborhood as he struggled to understand the perplexing reality around him. For most of his early childhood, Jakeem looked for avenues of escape from a large family living in close proximity in a small house. The basement of his home offered him a place of solitude. There, he would read for hours, removed from the confusion in his household. In the basement, Jakeem carved out a small space, bordered by storage boxes of treasured relics, a washing machine and dryer, tools, and a bicycle in need of repair. In this space, he read his books, safely distanced from the upstairs noises and the street beyond. Here, he had adventure, drama, and mystery.

"He hoped he would learn what his life could be like," said his mother. "He wanted not to be so withdrawn, so unhappy. It was family things. There were a lot of problems. He has deep thoughts."

When we think of Jakeem reading in his basement, we are reminded of Dewey's comment that language is a means for working through and understanding our world. Shadowed by the bulk of a washer and dryer, Jakeem worked through his struggles: the teasing at school, a troubled older brother, fear for the safety of his aggressive twin, the neighborhood gangs, and the poor who lived in his community. Today, Jakeem's thoughts about life have not changed that much. "I would like to help the poor," Jakeem said most recently. "When I would go to my grandmother's I saw a poor person. He was asking to pump her gas for her to get some money. It makes me feel bad when I see a poor person on the street."

As Jakeem advanced through elementary school, his quiet reading space changed, but his reasons for reading did not. As we observed Jakeem, we began to understand his mother's view of him as a reader and interpreter of the world. Safely sitting in his desk or on a cushion in a reading corner, Jakeem used reading as a way to confront his fears and take on the world. Soon after eight-year-old Jakeem joined our class, he sat at his desk and wrote the following journal entry about the book *Maniac Magee*:

> I wish I was Maniac Magee because I would have liked to have did all those things. Maniac they thought he was crazy. He wants to run away because he isn't wanted. If I was him I wouldn't run away because of one person [an insensitive adult who told the white child Maniac to leave a black neighborhood]. If I were Maniac I would have been glad to have helped someone like Grayson to learn how to read. And I would have been glad to have helped anyone else who would need my help.

Maniac was everything Jakeem wanted to be. Maniac dared to live on his own. He dared to help others and outwit the bullies in both the white and the black sections of town. He dared to live with a black family that treated him as an equal. Maniac also ran away from home, something Jakeem once considered but never attempted. Reading provided Jakeem with answers that helped him achieve peace of mind.

Jakeem read voraciously when he first entered our third-grade classroom, yet he realized that reading alone did not provide all the answers. He sensed a need to step beyond reading to understand and effect change in the world. Although reading contributed much to his life and growth, it was through writing that a more articulate, confident person emerged. Two years after he left grade school, Jakeem wrote a thank-you letter to a local merchant who donated to a fund to pay for the publication of a student anthology:

Dear Mr. Plath,

     My name is Jakeem. I was a shy kid, with a low self esteem. It was writing that gave me courage and raised my confidence in myself . . . Writing has become a very important part of my life. When I feel upset, writing is a way of cooling off. I often find myself thinking of stories that relate to everyday life. When I write about my life I can put the things I learn to use . . . It is because of your generosity that my stories and those of others are now able to reach kids city wide . . .

Gratefully,
Jakeem
Grade 7

In his letter, Jakeem mentions two purposes for writing: writing helped him with self-esteem, and reading it can help others. It is not difficult to imagine the thinking behind Jakeem's letter. He had learned a great deal by reading, so why couldn't others read what he wrote and learn from him? Jakeem writes to explore his ideas. Writing is a means of negotiating his life.

"Writing helps me release my feelings," Jakeem once told us. "I don't like just thinking about something. If it's something that makes me feel bad, I write it down. And if you really put your mind to it, somebody might have a change of heart." To explain what he meant, Jakeem commented about a story he wrote about the poor when he was nine. "I wish that it would change their [other children] lives and make it that they would help out the poor."

Yet despite all of the positive comments about writing Jakeem has shared with us over the years, it was during his presentation of "Beauty" to a classroom full of college students that he revealed his deepest feelings. He read his poem softly, with a subtle combination of awareness and passion.

BEAUTY

Beauty is a bee in a flower.
Beauty is a butterfly in the wind.
Beauty is in the summer.
Beauty is the animals in the woods.
Beauty is birds in the trees.
Beauty is a lake.

I wonder how it got there?
It's a mystery to me.

Beauty is everything around us . . .
and leaves falling.
But mostly love.

Beauty is pain in your heart
you can only call love.

Beauty is a baby being born.
Beauty is a mother holding her baby.
Beauty is life.

Beauty is a baby learning to walk

Beauty is on Valentine's Day

Beauty is love.

Amid the applause that followed Jakeem's dramatic reading, a collective question emerged. "Why did you write the poem?" He was ready with an answer. "I just wanted to write a poem. Especially when people are talking about war [Persian Gulf War] and stuff. Right now there's a lot of people getting hurt in the Middle East [several of Jakeem's classmates had relatives, including mothers and aunts, who participated in the war]. Instead of thinking about war, I thought about flowers and stuff. If you think about something good, maybe you'll have a good feeling about somebody coming home. I wanted other people to read my thoughts. Instead of thinking about something bad, to think about something good."

As Jakeem reflected on his poem, we noticed echoes of his mother's voice that took us back to those times in the basement when he read about good things, about possibilities. "He isn't a fighter. He is a positive kind of person. He has a calming disposition. A lot of times he has to calm me down." "Beauty" had that calming effect for Jakeem. The poem helped him and his classmates to understand a complex historical event.

Despite Jakeem's optimistic view of life and his willingness to share his feelings, "Emergency" served a somewhat different purpose. It was personal. At the time, inner struggles, old and new fears, had resurfaced. How would he tame those fears and bring them out into the open? Jakeem wrote nonstop for several days, and then one day asked us if we would read his narrative essay "in private." Silently, we read.

EMERGENCY

One day I stayed home from school because I was sick. My father was taking care of me. When my twin brother, Jacob, came home from school my older brother's friend, Ricky, wanted to see my older brother, Justin. My father wouldn't let Ricky come in because he knew he dealed crack and my brother Justin had gotten in trouble with him the day before.

On the day I was sick, Ricky came down to my house with his friend. This is how it happened. They were pulled over by the police, my big brother Justin was with them. The police found crack in the car so the car was confiscated so Ricky came down to my house to talk to my brother Justin, but my father wouldn't let him. He asked my father, "What's your problem?"

"I don't have a problem," said my father.

Ricky and his friend backed away from the house. Ricky started to shoot and hit the window and hit the stereo. He shot the kitchen and hit the cupboard. Jacob and I got down on the floor.

My mother came home from work. She is a teacher. My father told her what happened and they called the police. They came right over. The second time they shot they hit the door. My mother called the police at 9:30 P.M., but they didn't get there until 10:00 P.M.

We stayed with my grandfather until Friday. When I came home I was sick. My father got protection. Nothing has happened so far. I think of this scary memory all the time. It is really scary to me.

As we finished, Jakeem was looking at us intensely. "What do you think?" Our replies were awkward and ineffective. "This is a wonderful story. You are very brave to have written this. Is your brother OK now? Were you scared? Are you ready to share this with the class?"

Our last question startled him. "I would rather not," he said. At that moment, we realized the private, very personal nature of this story. Jakeem's writing of "Emergency" and our reading of the story were enough to provide relief from the hurtful experience he and his family had endured. As we soon discovered, however, Jakeem's private writing, like his private reading sessions in the basement, did not sustain his sense of relief. A few days later, Jakeem asked a small group of his classmates to read his story. At first, it was a painful experience for him, which we saw as a matter of being able to trust. But as the children gradually responded to "Emergency," Jakeem recognized his fears about the experience. It was a moment of enlightenment that bolstered his self-image. "Emergency" served as the "mean face" that Jakeem once adopted to scare away bullies in his neighborhood. In sharing "Emergency" with his classmates, Jakeem became more like his assertive twin, whom he admired—daring, adventurous, and fearless. "Emergency" was Jakeem's challenge to life: he would seek to control events rather than be controlled by them.

What Jakeem has learned is that writing—and sharing writing—can be a way of building self-confidence. This notion is made clearer in Jakeem's conversation with a visiting poet. We had invited Kente, an adult from the neighborhood, to share some of his poems with our children. Kente selected one called "Society" because he wanted to have an impact on students who confronted the issue of drug misuse in their community every day. "Society" touched a freshly exposed nerve in Jakeem.

"I recognize what you meant when you said people die because of the poisons they deal," said Jakeem. "I write as a way of getting things off [my] mind that bother me." In an aside, Jakeem cupped his hand and whispered to Vicki, "Someone hurt his feelings. In his heart. It sounds like he got rid of his hurt by writing."

Kente was sympathetic to Jakeem's response. As he explained, "We have to look past that system and change that system. When a system is not good, we must confront it."

"Most people in society are hurting [other] people and don't care what they do," replied Jakeem.

Kente added, "What I hope is that my writing will help people see the problem and recognize it in their own family."

Jakeem's response was barely audible. "I understand what you are saying. I have a brother who had a problem with drugs."

As we listened to Jakeem and Kente, we noted a fascinating parallel: Both used writing as a way to understand an intense, troubling experience. But more important, both discovered the power of their writing by making it public. Together, they represent the human potential to effect change through meaningful story. By writing—and sharing that writing with a receptive audience—they relieved themselves of some of the tension that threatened to control their lives.

Jakeem's experience with "Emergency" and his conversations with Kente are noteworthy because they enabled him to grow as an individual. But his continued growth did not depend on such experiences. He was constantly in search of more positive images of life. Now we understand why Jakeem, to this day, chooses "Beauty" rather than "Emergency" in his narratives and poems of himself. "Beauty" allows him to think beyond the present, and many of his classmates agree with his way of thinking. Jakeem had already come to realize that focusing too much on life's problems might distract him from what he considered most significant: the beauty in life.

In an empty classroom, one of our alternative spaces for conferring about writing, several children commented on "Emergency."

"It makes you mad," said Paul, "because he is always trying to get somebody in trouble, and then he shot up their house. They coulda' got shot. The beginning part kind of makes you happy. Like when he went out to his grandfather's house, but he needs to put some more good parts, because there's already enough bad stuff in the world. You don't want to read about people getting shot."

Like his fellow students, Jakeem does not want to play up the violence, he wants to play up the beauty of living. In his Reflection Journal, Jakeem quotes Plato, who was quoted in a biography Jakeem read: "At the touch of love everyone becomes a poet," an expression of Jakeem's developing philosophy of life.

When Jakeem wrote "Emergency" he was nine. He has seldom returned to the story since. Poetry has become the mainstay of his writing. Recently, Jakeem visited Vicki's fourth-grade classroom. As a thirteen-year-old writer, he shared his philosophy about writing and life with eight- and nine-year-olds. Once again, he celebrated "Beauty" in a reading. Then he settled in with other young authors to write. By the end of the day, Jakeem had crafted a new poem, one that expresses his growing confidence as an individual who sees the world in terms of possibility rather than obstacle.

A MAN

A man is one who cries in silence but thinks out loud.
A man is a person
who has a mind like a steal trap.
A man is a person
who has a body like a bear
but a heart and soul like a newborn baby.
A man is a person
who knows he can't do it alone,
so he has much respect for his wife and loved ones.

A man is scared
but is fearless to his family and the world.
A man doesn't need a gang or a gun,
if he does he's a coward.

A man is quiet
when the situation calls for a loud speaker.
A man will not fight physically,
but uses his mind to fight
and knows when to draw the line.
A man speaks his mind
but knows his soul.
A man can show his feelings among friends
and feel no less of a man.
A man compromises when it's necessary
but will not compromise his feelings.

A man respects the feelings of others at all times.

A man may be ignorant to the sensitivities of a woman
but will stop at nothing to learn and understand.
A man doesn't need to say anything to be understood.

And remember all boys grow to become men.

> Sometimes you must see with your heart
> and not with your eyes to understand.

Dana: She's My Hill

I'm white and I read this whole Dr. King book. "Hate can't drive out hate.
If you live by the sword; you die by the sword."

Donald Murray, an educator and writer, claims that all writing is autobiographical. From our experience with young writers, we would agree with Murray's general premise. We seldom read a child's writing—a journal, poem, song, or story—that doesn't yield evidence of the child's life history. For example, Dana's journal entry (quoted above) reveals her evolving philosophy of life. She is white, living and attending school in an African American community. And she is interested in preserving peace through peaceful means, having been deeply affected by the teachings of a great black leader. Her writing is both informative and imaginative and captures her individual uniqueness. In many ways,

Dana is like all the children we teach who reveal themselves through what they do and what they write about. But she is much different as a writer. She is one of the few children we know who consciously incorporates her own socially aware philosophy in almost everything she writes. This awareness, which Dana brought to our class, blossomed during the two years she was one of our students.

Working on one of her first stories for our class one day, Dana sits wistfully at her desk. The pencil in her right hand becomes a drumstick: vertical strokes tap out a rhythm on the blank piece of paper. A story develops. The drumstick becomes a pencil again, and horizontal strokes give shape to a new story.

I think I want to be a rapper when I grow up. My favorite woman rap singer is M. C. Lyte. She's my itill. I want to be just like her when I grow up. She doesn't say a lot of nasty words when she raps. Sometimes she raps about drugs. I think more people should listen to her song CADICHINE. At the end she says, LEAVE THE DRUGS ALONE!

At first, Dana's tribute to rap barely got our attention. We didn't take it seriously. Eventually, however, we realized that her writing was not just a whimsical salute to a rap idol. Dana related to rappers like M. C. Lyte because she exercised her powerful woman's voice to expose drugs as an insidious evil. But writing about others who effect change was not enough for Dana. She imagined herself as one of those whose voice could affect others and wrote her own rap.

YO BROS

What's your name?
You know school an't a game.
Your there to learn not to play.
Sometimes schools are out for the day.
DON'T be writing on no walls,
DON'T be playing in no halls,
DON'T be calling people names,
DON'T bring weapons and guns to school.
Yo bro that's a wrong thing to do.
And if you want to be cool
STAY IN SCHOOL

31

For Dana, rap and writing are powerful tools for staking out her position in the world. Among other things, nine-year-old Dana's rap gave voice to her own political identity. The intensity of rap provided a perfect medium. It captured her emotions as a human being, her commitment to understanding social and political issues, and her sense of responsibility for social change.

Such intensity reappears in what looks like a casual rap about one of Dana's favorite idols.

> Dr. Martin Luther King
> Worked very hard in this world
> For peace, justice, and nonviolence.
> Now he's dead
> And every January
> We remember his birthday.

Dr. King is the perfect subject for Dana's early writings. She respected his efforts because he brought blacks and whites together. For Dana, Dr. King was not dead and gone. He dedicated his life to a social cause that changed people's lives. Through her rap poems, Dana began to realize the power of the written word to achieve change. Writing was like listening to rap. It was a performance that inspired interesting thoughts in both the writer and the reader. Writing created a space for this performance to occur. It allowed her not only to explore and proclaim her views and her ideals, but to express herself in relation to these values.

From listening to rap, Dana turned to reading biographies and autobiographies of strong women who helped others at the risk of their own lives. Sojourner Truth, Harriet Tubman, and Winnie Mandela became her new models. They were crusaders for human rights. One morning, in response to a class reading of Winnie Mandela's prison diary, Dana wrote in her journal,

> I think more people should read and write. Without the knowledge of reading and writing I don't think people will do that much . . . I learned that she got fired from a lot of jobs because she was married to him [Nelson Mandela]. Her children couldn't go to school, and she was banned cause they had a ban law from school for her children. And she doesn't use bad words. She doesn't fight. She fights for freedom.

We don't know how much Dana already sensed about the power of autobiographical writing to transform the writer, but we do know one thing Winnie Mandela's diary taught Dana: through writing, a person can not only examine social and political issues but express a personal position in relation to those issues. Winnie Mandela wrote about oppression and injustice, but she also wrote about her commitment to change. This kind of autobiographical writing became a model for Dana, who assumed the role of a subjective writer. It was of no consequence to her that she might reveal bits of herself through her writing. She preferred it that way. Hadn't Mandela and King revealed themselves through their writings and speeches? They took a stand and were recognized for it. So would she. Soon after, Dana wrote her most ambitious autobiographical narrative, "The Free Program," which embodied her philosophy of life and of writing.

On one of the first days of school, Dan picked up a sweater left behind by a student. "Whose is it?" he asked. All eyes took in the sweater, a well-worn dacron knit, faded brown and grey. Three small buttons were matched to stretched and frayed buttonholes. As soon as Dan asked the question, he knew it was a mistake. Whoever owned the sweater was not proud that they were poor. Who would want to own up to such an unstylish, telltale garment? He draped the sweater over a chair in the back of the room.

During the lunch break, as we sat together in the classroom, there was a knock at the door. "I just wanted to ask you something," Dana whispered to us. It was a question about her homework. We answered the question and went back to our lunch, thinking that Dana would return to the playground. Instead, she moved quietly toward the back table. Slowly she reached for the sweater, then turned and moved quickly out the door.

Several months after the sweater incident, Vicki e-mailed Dan.

> Dana expressed an interest in beginning her own shelter for the poor. Dana emphasized that she has not been in a shelter, but her mom has used the services of Focus Hope. She said they bought food there a lot: cheese, butter, flour, rice, and canned foods. I know Focus Hope has been a government distribution center for many years.

We discovered that the program Dana referred to was indeed a government distribution center, but one unlike most of those found throughout the city. Focus Hope enjoys worldwide recognition as a community program that assists unemployed poor families. They have also reclaimed several industrial buildings and blocks of property in a low socioeconomic area of the city. Fewer than ten years ago, abandoned buildings lined a half-mile stretch that is now the property of Focus Hope. As an infant, Dana took her first steps along those blocks of crumbled, weed-choked sidewalks and abandoned buildings, where broken windows and leaking roofs discouraged entry.

As a four-year-old, Dana witnessed the neighborhood's transformation. Focus Hope now occupies these postwar structures. Professionals and technical experts (many of them volunteers) retrain unemployed residents as machinists and design engineers. Classrooms occupy an upper floor, where teachers assist adults in acquiring their G.E.D. A food distribution center serves pregnant mothers, their infants, and young children. A modern Montessori Day Care Center is showcased at the entrance to the complex. It was at Focus Hope that a young Dana dropped food into a supermarket basket and watched at the counter as clerks respectfully packed her mom's groceries and loaded them into a waiting car.

The image of her neighborhood now and her neighborhood then was clearly on Dana's mind when she began to write.

THE FREE PROGRAM

I see commercials and programs on T.V. where people ask you to give money to the people who don't have a place to live, enough food to eat, or can't go to school. They also ask you to give money so the people can go to doctors and hospital for medicine and treatment. I think that people should give the people who don't have these things but need them and can't do these things but need to, all the things they need free and let them do all the things they need to free.

I know if the people could get these things free and do these things free that the people or places and people who work there wouldn't get paid. But I think there should be a program for the people who need these things but don't have them, and for the people who need to do these things but can't. The program is for: people who need to do these things but can't; and people who need these things but don't have them. These people will get these things free. And the people who can do these things and don't need to be in the program shouldn't be in it.

If the program is accepted into business, I will accept all colors, races, sizes, ages, adults, babies, children, teenagers—and old people, real old people—and everyone who needs to be in the program be in it.

> Also, if the program is accepted into business, the people who will work at the program won't be working there for money. They will be working there because they know they're helping someone. I wouldn't get paid. No one would. The program will have rooms that look like apartments if the people need a place to stay or live. The program will also have food, drinks, clothes, doctors, a hospital and pharmacy, a school inside for everyone who wants to go to school. Everything the program gives or lets you do is free.

Dana knew her story would cause a stir in the classroom, just as Winnie Mandela's diary had for her several weeks earlier. When she read it in class, the other children didn't disappoint her. They were confused, but their interest was piqued. Shanette's voice dominated the others as they worked to get Dana's attention. "In the story it says I will do all these things. I want to do all. I want all these things to happen. But how will she make all of these things happen without money?"

Dana was in control. She pointed out that businesses would help. She reminded Shanette to look in her story. "It's there," said Dana.

Paul supported her. "It's something for the government and the president to think about instead of Donald Trump, instead of buying them [the poor] old rich motels and stuff." Paul, who struggled in school because of his poor reading and writing skills, expressed our sentiments perfectly. In her essay, Dana articulated a philosophy of giving respect to those who are in financial need. As Paul noted, that in itself is something to celebrate. But Dana also positioned herself in her story as a person who is willing to take responsibility for creating and even implementing such a generous program.

For Dana, "The Free Program" served as a test case. In the process of writing and presenting her essay, she took action in relation to a social cause that was important to her. She discovered that she could move others to think about social issues. Her experience in writing "The Free Program" enabled her to grow as a conscientious and responsible person. She learned how to commit herself to such issues and to identify openly with them. Dana grew as a writer and an individual through her success in writing "The Free Program" and discussing it in class.

Dana's early success in our classroom, as a writer and an advocate for social change, does not alone define her. As we have said, it is the accumulation of writing and action of a child that gives us a full profile of a child as a writer. Dana did not stop developing as a writer. Soon after her presentation of "The Free Program," Dana recruited her mother to collaborate with her. They wrote an essay about the Persian Gulf War that was to be the cornerstone of a dozen or so stories and poems written by other children.

NO MORE WARS PLEASE

We don't need to go to war. Too many lives have been lost in other wars like the war between the North and the South, World War I, and World War Two. There is enough people losing their lives without having another war. Innocent people just being in the wrong place at the wrong time. Another war would not only hurt and kill our soldiers it will also bring harm and anger to the others left here in the states. There will be a great deal of anger. People blaming people for this and that. Putting the blame on everyone.

But there is no one to blame. Everyone should try to come together as one (to come together and unite and be strong). Working together is better than being alone. Working together as one we could solve many things. Fighting isn't going to solve anything. The worst thing of all is the innocent people are going to get hurt. Babies and children who know nothing are going to be killed. The ones who can't fight for themselves will be killed. Why? Just because of man's greed. Let the children be children. Let them live. Let them decide when they are grown enough to understand. Let them decide. Don't kill them in their prime. Why? Why fight? Why kill innocent people and children? As Martin Luther King, Jr. said, "All men are created equal." Also as John Lennon said, "Give peace a chance." Stop fighting. No more wars please.

Dana's commitment continues to intrigue us. Although we have encountered other children her age who act as advocates and write about similar issues, very few of our students see themselves as full-time advocates. We are left to wonder why. Perhaps children are aware of the pressure social activists face in standing up for causes and don't want to stick out in the crowd. What we have learned is that children like Dana, who use their writing and oral skills to work for social change, dare to be different, despite what others might say.

Once, in responding to Dan's inquiry about a popular book all the children fought to read, Dana said, "Sometimes it is funny. But when a book makes me sleepy, I think: I have more responsibility! I have a lot of work to do!" Each morning, while her mother is at work, Dana gets her younger brother and sister ready for school. And each day after school, Dana walks her brother and sister safely home. Dana is drawn to books that fictionalize real-life events. She values literature that introduces topics she will later talk and write about. These are the books that have staying power for Dana and contribute ideas to her autobiographical reflections.

We recall an incident that took place in the first semester of Dana's fourth-grade year. One of our students, Jerome, wrote that he and his friends shot firecrackers at power lines and watched the sparks fly. Raymond matched the story with his adventures on Devil's Night, when he threw eggs at a neighbor's windows. Neither seemed to see any problem with their activities. They had done it in fun. As a class, we talked about Jerome's story and Raymond's story and our reactions. We were on familiar ground. Not long before, our city had received national attention. We were labeled "out of control" during the nights preceding Halloween. Hundreds of arsonists' fires lit up the sky—fires that resulted in millions of dollars in property damage. As the fires raged, so did the citizens. The mayor and city council had given serious attention to the city's youth. They organized block clubs to take the city back from the vandals. They enforced curfews. As our class discussion progressed, voices rose, some in opposition to Jerome's story and some suggesting the harmlessness of such activities. Dana's protests were loudest, but in the end nothing much was settled. Or so we thought.

As time passed, the Devil's Night discussion worked on Dana. She often let her ideas brew for a while before she advanced them in conversation and writing. We should have recognized that the Devil's Night issue was not over. It presented her with an opportunity to define herself and her thinking further. One year after the class discussion, Vicki e-mailed Dan:

> This afternoon the Hutchinson family came to visit my classroom. They were proud of Dana's picture with the Mayor and the radio announcer. Framed in the picture was Dana, standing next to the most powerful mayor her city ever had. Yet she seemed not as out of place as her nine-year-old body would suggest. She stood proud with a winning essay that shouted to the citywide audience: "Stop fires before they start. Protect the people. Act now!"

Several years have passed since Dana was last in our class, yet we continue to hear her voice and read about her life as a social advocate.

Recently, Dana called Vicki. "Hello, Mrs. Rybicki? It's Dana. You won't believe what I've written! Read tomorrow's newspaper. I'm in it."

Indeed she was. Leo Manor was dead and two police officers were being sent to jail for second-degree murder. Were the trial and convictions justified? asked the opinion-page editor. Dana was one of the guest writers who had responded. She wrote

A VICTIM OF SOCIETY

Leo Manor was a victim of a society in which police officers are supposed to make us feel safe. The police who were supposed to protect Leo Manor beat him to death. How safe does that make us feel?

We are fortunate to have learned so much from Dana. Putting together her profile has provided us with tremendous insights on children's ability to write provocatively and to position themselves in relation to a cause they think just. For children like Dana, writing becomes a way to etch themselves and their ideas into the minds of others. And for Dana especially, writing is a means not so much of letting others know where you come from but where you are going.

Kevin: The Trauma of Separation

I see Kevin every day, and when I read his story it seems like he's not the same child. He's got a lot of energy. When I see, and when I read this it almost brings me to tears. He's lost both parents. He's separated, you know, from his mother. In a way he says he's got an understanding of what's going on. It's very interesting that he's holding up so well . . . It's like his story is some kind of therapy for him and it's his way of telling everyone "It's fine." He is fine.

Dan listened as Jackie, a classroom assistant in Vicki's third- and fourth-grade split class, explained her morning's interaction with Kevin. His story moved her. "I'm not sure I know the real Kevin," she said.

Dan thought back to the day Kevin entered Vicki's classroom, late in the fall of the previous year. He was taller than the other children and slumped unceremoniously at his desk most of that morning. In Vicki's class, children new to the school are usually introduced by their parents or care-givers. Kevin was not. He seemed alone and dejected. On Day Two, Kevin's uncle, a large man with soothing eyes, knocked on the classroom door. He apologized for interrupting the class, then hesitated as he looked around at the eight- and nine-year-olds staring up at him from their writing workshop clusters. Sensing his apprehension, Vicki escorted him to a more private corner of the room. Mr. Seller spoke in a loud voice: "Kevin should not be in fourth grade. I would rather he be in the third grade."

Vicki was caught off guard for a moment but managed to motion Mr. Seller out into the hallway. Mr. Seller explained, "We just got Kevin and his brother. I don't know how long this is going to last, but last year was a hard year for him. He had a terrible report card with D's and F's. He will not be able to do the next grade's work with those marks. So even though the school passed him, I asked in the office if he could be in third grade."

Vicki agreed and explained to Mr. Seller that she would make the proper change in the office and in her record book. But she also asked him if she could tell Kevin in her own way, to protect his self-esteem.

As Vicki reentered her classroom, her immediate concern was Kevin. The whole class had heard Mr. Seller's request. *Students put curses on classmates who "fail" and so do parents!* Vicki thought. After sending Kevin to the office to retrieve some book supplies, Vicki addressed the inquisitive students. She explained that what Kevin's uncle thought was best for Kevin should be respected. "Kevin needs your support."

As it turned out, Kevin's classmates were a great source of moral support for him. His grade change never seemed to come up again in class, most likely because third and fourth graders often sat next to one another during writing and reading workshops, and because Vicki refused to make a big deal out of the situation. And although he struggled with his reading when he first arrived in class, methodically using his finger to trace words, his classmates read with him and encouraged him. By the second semester, they were impressed. They considered him intelligent because of his insightful comments about difficult ideas. In turn, they provided an atmosphere of trust—an atmosphere where Kevin could grow without fear of being judged too harshly. In many ways, Kevin's classmates, like his aunt and uncle, provided a safe home for him. He yearned for such an environment.

Even as a new student, Kevin wanted to talk about his "family problems," as he often called them. He felt confident that our classroom offered him a forum in which to share his personal history. In our classroom, Kevin could do private writing and make part, or all, of that writing public when he chose. At first he chose to share his family stories only with peers in small groups, but eventually many of his ideas about family, especially the foster care family situation he was a part of, became chosen topics for his writing and for larger classroom discussions.

Jackie interrupted Dan's thoughts. "Have you read Kevin's story?" Yes, he had. It was a story that had a familiar ring. Instinctively, he leaned over the sheet of paper Jackie held respectfully in her hand and slowly he took it in. One more time.

Two years ago I came to live with my uncle. On that day he put me in a certain class that encouraged me to write stories. One day in the middle of the school year I went home and told my uncle I had wrote a story. My uncle was proud of me writing. Now I have a new story to share with you about my life.

THE PHONE CALL

One day when I was watching t.v. the phone rang and I picked it up. I was surprised with who it was until I was talking to her. It was my mother. I was happy so I asked her where are you and she said, 'I am in the state of Kentucky.' I told her when I am 19 I will come to see you.

She is still in Kentucky as I speak and I think about how it has been to be separated from my mom since I was five years old.

Me as a little boy it is sometimes hard for me because when I was at my old house the other kids talked about us. Sometimes the bigger boys picked on my brother and one day my foster cousins came and beat a boy up. That is how hard it is being separated from my mother and father.

I can also say that if it was not for my caring uncle and auntie I will not have contact with my family. They love me like a real mother and father so all can say that I am blessed and I love them very much because they try to do what they can.

My father loves me but I do not know what he is saying. Me and my brother have to get over that my father is in jail. Sometimes I pretend I am my father and I am so tall that a ball is an ant. I miss my father and I hope he misses me too.

I think about all my friends in class and special people who help me with my problem.

As Dan finished reading, Jackie asked, "Do you think it would be OK to talk to Kevin about his story?"

"Sure."

Jackie's request seemed natural. She respected the children as authors—writers who share their insights on living in a world that is often confusing, sometimes funny, and always complex. Her curiosity about Kevin's story was not unlike that of any other inquisitive student in the class who had read his story. And, like other members of the class, Jackie was used to playing the role of a reader who had questions for an author. Besides, Kevin probably anticipated talking more about his story.

"What is the rest of the story?" Jackie said to Dan as she moved away.

Dan watched as Jackie and Kevin squeezed into a couple of small chairs nearby. Her first words to Kevin hovered in the air: "This story made me interested. I see you every day and I think you handle the separation very well." She paused for a moment. "I have a question, and you don't have to answer if you don't want to. Do you understand why you are separated?"

Kevin absorbed her words without speaking.

"You're not the only sibling that had to go with your uncle."

"Yes."

Jackie tried to find the right words to explain to Kevin the benefits of the risk he took in writing his story. "If you continue to write like this, you can go far. Lovely story. I can feel all the feelings in the story. I think if a lot of people read this story they would be happy and know that they could overcome a lot of things. And . . ."

Suddenly his eyes misted and words burst from Kevin: "The reason I wrote this story was because all the years I went through without my mother and father I just wanted to forget about them and just leave them behind. Because I know someday I'll be able to see them."

"You don't have to forget them, because they are still your parents," Jackie responded.

"I'm just talking about the separation. I don't want to forget them."

Jackie thought for a moment. "It's good that you are doing all right with it. A lot of children . . . (hmmmm) . . . have a lot of anger . . . (ahhh) . . . when these things happen. And I think you are handling it well. But if you need to talk about it, I think you should do that. Anytime!"

Kevin's story baffled Jackie. It was what he *didn't* write about that interested her, that which she thought was implicit in his written words. The smiling face she saw almost every day in class was not an image she recognized in Kevin's story. Why? She wanted to know more, but her time with Kevin ran out. Another classroom. More children to work with. For a long moment, Jackie stared into Kevin's eyes. "Thank you for letting me go through this story and talk to you about it."

On her way out of the room, Jackie spoke quietly to Dan: Kevin seemed eager to talk more. It was an opening Dan had been looking for since the previous year. He had been intrigued that Kevin was upbeat and optimistic about life, yet on the inside struggled with recurring fears about separation. *Reality appears to be closer to what you read or hear in a person's story than what you see in their actions in daily life,* he thought. Like Jackie, Dan was curious about what was on Kevin's mind.

Dan saw Kevin working on his story and slid into the empty chair next to him. "What were you two talking about?"

"She was just asking about how hard it was for me getting separated from my mother and father. I told her I wanted to write about them because I wanted to forget it."

"But when you write, does it really make you forget?"

"I write it down and I try thinking about what I wrote. I go home." Kevin stopped and shifted in his seat. " 'Cause sometimes my brother he cry because" [another brief pause] "he don't like me writing about how we got separated. He told me not to write and I said I want to forget it. And he said if you write it, if you forget, that's what he was going do."

It appeared to Dan that Kevin's brother was satisfied with his answer. Kevin didn't have to explain how writing helped, it just did. "Then this summer I wrote my first story and he started writing what he wanted to forget, and I told him that anything he wanted to forget he should try to write it down."

Dan's mind drifted for a moment. He was reminded once again of others, including children from Vicki's class, who used storytelling and story writing to clear their minds. Through their stories, they faced difficult issues. Stories offered openings for action rather than passive acceptance of present circumstances.

"So you write it down?"

"And I just go play or something, and then I forget about it."

"You kind of get it off your chest? . . . then you don't have to keep thinking about it because it is down on paper?" Dan's own questions came back at him. Can writing get rid of the pain by transferring it to paper? Did Kevin believe this? Did Dan?

Altering the focus, Dan continued, "You let your brother read some of your writing. And so, when he read it, he didn't like you writing about it?"

"He liked my story and . . ." Kevin stopped. He remembered something important, distant. "He don't like me sharing how we got to foster homes and stuff. I forget a lot of stuff . . . I even forgot I had another story until I came into class this year."

Kevin's digression confused Dan at first, but then proved valuable and timely. Although his brother was indeed on Kevin's mind when he wrote "The Phone Call" and when he was talking with Dan, it was a story Kevin had written the year before, in third grade, that had provoked the vociferous response from his brother. And it was that story, and Kevin's experience with it, that provided much of the context for Kevin's answers.

The year before, Vicki sent Dan an e-mail message saying that Kevin had written a powerful story in response to his reading: he felt lost without his parents, and he had been hurt by so many moves. His aunt and uncle were surprised, and his uncle went to class to talk to Vicki about it. He couldn't believe that Kevin had written this story on his own—Kevin, for whom his previous teacher had recommended special education. He leaned closer to see the writing on the desk in front of Vicki, the story Kevin referred to in introducing "The Phone Call."

AS MY LIFE TURNS

In the summertime I had fun but when it rains I didn't have too much fun and when it stops I run outside. I played with my dogs but when I have to go in I play with my brother.

When I was four years old I was separated from my mother and father. My brother and I were crying in the car that day. When I was eight my brother and I were afraid we were going to be separated from each other but we were saved by my uncle and auntie. They took us into adoption. Now they are our mother and father.

My brother and I do everything together. Sometimes we have a little bit of disagreement. It is happy that my brother and I live together and have each other too.

Focusing back on his conversation with Kevin, Dan realized that "The Phone Call" functioned as an extension of "As My Life Turns." It was understandable then that Kevin's responses to questions about "The Phone Call" would be constructed from the context of his entire lived experience.

"Your brother was worried that you were talking about the separation. Do you mean because others might be reading about it?"

"Yeah," said Kevin. "And they might make fun of us."

"Have you found that to be true?"

"No, because the people in section 7 [peer teachers] and sec 3 [our class]—everyone is my friend here. And they help me to forget about it. Jerrod, he tells me to forget about it. He tells me to write about something else, a funny story or something. My brother knows that I have a lot of friends and they help me and some of his friends help him because every time someone makes fun of him he loses his temper. Like, if some talks about his mother, our mother, he gets mad."

Talking and writing. For Kevin they had a lot in common. Both in and out of the classroom these forms of expression invited "friends" into a conversation important to Kevin and his brother. In the process, these friends helped to soothe the anger both of them had.

Dan pointed to a sentence in "The Phone Call." "Look what you wrote here: 'about all my friends in class and special people who help me with my problem.' You think it is a problem?"

"Yeah."

"Tell me about your closeness to your brother."

"We live mostly our whole lives together. We love each other and we stay together no matter what. Like, if he's in trouble with my uncle, I try to help him so I'm in trouble with him."

"How long have you lived with your uncle?"

"About two years."

"Do you think all brothers have a special bond like you and your brother? How did you ever get that close?"

"We had our own room. And anytime anyone wanted to come in, we had a secret word. Every time I think about it [separation], I think about our old house."

His house. Dan considered this new link. It occurred to him that Kevin's whole conversation with him and with Jackie had been held together by a series of links. In conversation, Kevin moved in and out of his past and present worlds: multiple images.

"One day I had this dream about our house. I didn't really know whose house it was until I asked my mother. And I guessed my own brother's name [a younger brother]. I asked her was our carpet blue? We had a big house. It had white walls. About five rooms. It was seven kids. And then that night they came and took my little brother away from us. That's the day when my mother just come home with my little brother, and we was going to teach him the little password."

Kevin's next words seemed forced. "But that night they took us away."

Dan recalled the request Kevin repeated often during the first year he came to live with his uncle and aunt. His one appeal to all who would listen was that he and his brother should never be separated. It was a passionate conviction that appeared to drive much of his behavior both in and out of class. Kevin's brother was his security and Kevin fiercely protected that security. As Dan sat with Kevin, he began to understand. Vicki had often told him about her own experience as a foster care parent of six boys over a fifteen-year period.

"When the boys first came to us, they had a constant fear of being, as they saw it, abandoned again. When we had to go grocery shopping, they questioned us. 'Are you coming back?' Three of our foster children frequently reminisced about their family. They talked about the disorganization of their home, their father's alcoholism, and his abusiveness. They described how they sometimes leaned out on a cold window ledge late at night, peeking to see if their mom was coming home. The little boys were left alone with their twelve-year-old sister, who cried as she waited too.

"It didn't help the situation that periodically, and by law, the Social Service Agency advertised the children for adoption in the local daily newspaper. Our children talked often about how they did not want to leave our care, yet they were angry with us when they read the ads. They assumed we wanted to get rid of them. Considering the instability in their life previous to arriving at our home, we understood their mistrust. However, it was no less difficult to swallow."

Kevin stood up briefly and then sat down again, tucking his leg under him. He was pensive. Dan had a faint idea of what he might be thinking. Kevin's life with his aunt and uncle was not always positive. He had spent a year trying to come to terms with his living arrangement. When he and his brother first arrived in their uncle's home, they were resistant. At the time, Kevin's uncle and Vicki talked at the classroom door every few weeks.

"Times were difficult at home and school for Kevin," Mr. Seller confided in Vicki. He seldom indicated the nature of incidents at home but often threw up his arms saying that he didn't know how long they could continue.

Vicki understood. "Our own children were often selfish in their need for attention," she told Mr. Seller. And then she added, "They longed for the dysfunctional family they had been taken from, fantasizing that their parents' homes were great, even though they knew of the difficulties. The children wanted us, as foster care-givers, to prove that we loved them. On the outside they appeared ungrateful, unforgiving, and unhappy. They did mean and mischievous things to test our endurance and love. Would we send them elsewhere if they were bad enough? How much would we take before they were given away—again?"

Anticipating Mr. Seller's concern about Kevin's education, Vicki told him that it was often most difficult for the children during the school day. "Sometimes evenings and mornings were so traumatic for our children, it was unpredictable what would follow in the classroom. We were teachers at the grade school and the high school our foster children attended, yet we were constantly in conference with the teachers. The teachers were supportive and understanding, but the children were not sympathetic. They seldom made it to school with the materials and homework we watched them place in their bookbags when they left. One son became irritated in school and slapped me across the face in reaction to a disciplinary comment I made to him. And I was his teacher!"

During these hallway meetings with Mr. Seller, Vicki confirmed that Mr. Seller meant more to Kevin than Kevin would lead him to believe. "Having kin for foster parents is very special to Kevin," she said. In Vicki's own experience her foster sons were always curious about their biological dad's whereabouts. And one son constantly talked about how he would change his mother's life after he got a good education and could provide for her. A few of her boys looked for a way out of the foster care home Vicki and her husband provided. They surreptitiously asked their social worker contacts when they would be allowed to look at their records so they could find their parents. Abandonment was a constant concern, and their search caused constant tensions. Yet with constant love they survived.

Vicki offered some friendly advice. "In the end, Kevin will see you in a very positive light. Twenty years after our last foster child left home, they continue to recognize each other and Paul and me as family. Our sons consider their relationships with each other and us as close as 'natural kin'." Before leaving, Mr. Seller smiled broadly at Vicki's reassurance, hoping that she was right.

Kevin's familiar smile returned to his face as Dan asked him one last question. "Can you tell me about your aunt and uncle?"

"I like living with them because they provide things for us. My uncle is a police officer and my aunt is a bus driver. Sometimes when she goes to work she takes us with her. Not on a school day. My uncle, he let us go to the terminal."

As if on cue, Kevin said he had to go. Upbeat, he picked up his story and walked back to his desk. Dan's eyes followed him. He thought for a moment and then wrote fondly in his journal:

> It's the same old Kevin that Jackie noticed every day. Thank goodness that he got to tell his story and that so many people are interested. Perhaps Jackie was right, stories are therapeutic. I wonder if his uncle has noticed the change?

Nora and Friends: Facing Dreams

Nora's voice, sharp and high-pitched, echoed above the others in her group. "Don't you see it?" Dan couldn't help but notice Nora. She towered above the others and demanded attention by her quickness, her frequent outbursts, and her mastery of language. He moved inconspicuously toward Nora's group, clustered together talking excitedly and writing. But by the time he was in position to listen in on their conversation, the voices died down and were silent. Nora's eyes were wide. She was tense. Three other children sat with blank stares. Then, as if on command, they blurted out a flurry of words in hurried, dissonant voices. Through it all Dan heard a dominant question. "Were you scared?"

And then it was over. The sound of the bell interrupted the writing group, and they dispersed in different directions. Dan stopped Nora at the door. "Would you mind talking with me about the discussion you and your friends had today?" Nora was always cautious with adults, but she consented.

The next morning Nora met with Dan in the hallway, a space we often used to extend the boundaries of our classroom and the writing workshop. She sat on the floor with her back against a locker-lined wall and brought her legs up to her chest. Several children walked by, lost in their own conversation. Nora leaned her head on her knees and began to talk in a low voice. Her father's fatal accident in September had haunted her for several weeks. There were vivid flashbacks. Screams. The funeral. Nora explained that she wanted to write a story that described her flashbacks, but her writing group did not understand what she was trying to do. She recalled the previous day's conversation. "I didn't understand . . . none of the people outside saw it happening. My father was coming towards me with blood on his body, and his face was scarred up, and I was scared."

Nora was confused. The flashbacks were so real to her, so threatening. She didn't understand why her friends couldn't see them as well. She thought that anyone who was close to her might also experience what she did in her dreams: the sight of her father as he emerged from the accident. She expected, or maybe wanted, her friends to see what she did and help her imagine a better way to deal with the situation. But they didn't. We didn't ask Nora whether she also expected us to experience the flashbacks, although it would seem reasonable for her to expect the same of us.

As we reflect on Nora's actions during the first part of the school year, we remember how unaffected Nora seemed when the tragedy occurred in late September, and we dismissed it as a significant event in her life. By late September her class involvement was the best it had been all year. She was vocal in discussing issues she had read about in large group formats. We were excited about her prospects as a dynamic learner. By early October, however, she was in a tailspin. Her moods isolated her from others. We tried giving her space. But it was not until the disruption in the writing group that we understood the full extent of her struggles.

In retrospect, we should not have been confused by Nora's mercurial behavior. We now see her response as that of a child who seeks to confront and understand the fears that haunt her. Children are often profoundly affected by the events that occur in their personal lives, and it is unlikely that they can entirely remove themselves from those situations while they are at school. Sylvia Ashton-Warner, an influential teacher of New

Zealand's Maori children in the 1950s and 1960s, says that children need spaces in which to express their fears, and that school and writing can provide such spaces. Like this pioneering educational reformer, we too have found that school should be a place of opportunity for children—a place where things that bother them might get worked out through various forms of language expression. And, given time and room, we try to assist with innovative ways to achieve solutions to their problems. Such was the case with Nora. In an effort to deal with her struggles, she wrote about her father's death and read about others who had suffered similar losses. If we had attended to the obvious behavioral signals Nora was giving us, we might not have been surprised when we overheard her say "I was scared." In fact, we might have been able to help her with her fears much sooner than we did.

What follows is a unique look at how a child uses story to understand the loss of a loved one. Our narrative also includes the stories of others who needed and used stories as Nora did. Any story, by its very nature, creates spaces for the intervening voices of others to enter and emerge. In fact, stories demand this. They are not as neat as we once imagined. Nora's story represents a composite of many children's stories—stories that seek to express the fear and resolve the mystery of death.

Immediately after her father's accident, Nora masked her true feelings. We saw an enthusiastic Nora, but she was immersed in fear. Her flash-backs—or dreams, as she sometimes referred to them—had begun in earnest. She struggled to understand their meaning. At the same time, she began to hear echoes of her loss in the stories of other children. She listened hard. In looking back at her Reflection Journal, we see evidence of the stories she had been listening to. Three weeks after her father's accident, and just before she introduced the idea of writing about her flash-backs to the writing group, Nora took a moment to reflect on her reading of "Buddy's Dream," a story from *Night on Neighborhood Street*.

I thought that Buddy had a strange dream and it was funny. I wonder why did he have such a dream?
P.S. I had a dream and it came true. It was about my father. He got killed in a car accident. My father was big and tall. He had two people in the back seat, and he saved them. And two days later, it happened. I was very sad and I cried for five days, and got over it. But I still cry once in awhile, only when someone says his name.

> . . . I would tell you, but even if I say it I will cry. Well, I have to take a chance. If you all promise not to say it. It's Raymond. Please don't say it or I'm telling Mrs. Rybicki.

As her reflections indicate, stories like "Buddy's Dream" reinforced for her the idea that dreams are part of human experience. Nora could relate to Buddy and his dreams. But as a written story, "Buddy's Dream" also gave Nora an idea: writing might be a way to negotiate the fears that threatened her. How had her father died? Would children in her class make fun of her tragedy?

In an interview about her journal entry, Nora recalled, "I got an idea [about writing] from a story I read. It was about a little boy, and he had a dream. His dream was weird. I thought about the dream that I had . . . I started writing about the dreams that I had . . . that my father got hurt in a car accident." Nora's comments were revealing. If someone else could write about strange dreams, then so could she. Soon afterwards, she completed a first draft of "Flashback" and introduced the topic to her writing group. It was their heated exchange Dan overheard. We were all brought face to face with the fears Nora had previously confronted alone.

For Nora, introducing the story to her friends was only a beginning. It barely touched her real fears. At her friend's urging, Nora expanded on her draft.

"You have to get it all out," Tamara said at the time.

Still, it was not easy for Nora. She was bursting with emotion and often cried when she met sympathetic classmates. Two weeks after the discussion, as she struggled to write more than one paragraph describing one of her flashbacks, she turned to a student anthology published several years earlier by a former fourth-grade class. Of particular interest to her was Allen's story "Good Times, Bad Times." Allen had written about the passing, in separate incidents, of both his mother and his father, and how their deaths triggered his bad behavior in school. He missed them very much. He included stories his aunt had shared with him about her own experiences when her parents died. For Allen, sharing was a form of recovery. He described how he changed because he wrote about his parents. In his anthology story, Nora read,

> I changed . . . by letting my feelings out when I wrote it on paper, and when I let other people know how did it feel to be lonely without your par-

ents. One day I helped this girl in my class. She had went through a bad
time about her mom and dad.

For several days, Nora read and reread Allen's story. She was genuinely
moved by his candidness, and by his discovery of the value of writing about
one's fears. Nora commented, "His mother and father got burned up in
a house fire, and he wrote it down, and he felt better. He said, 'You write
it on paper and you'll feel better about it.' "

Our own interpretation of Allen's story and his writing process paral-
lels Nora's. For Allen, writing meant that he could uncover the fears that
influenced the way he acted at home and at school, and by uncovering his
fears he could change.

To capture the full impact of what Nora internalized and intuited from
Allen's story, and to understand that her fear of death is a common fear
among children, we return to the fall of 1990. At that time Vicki wrote
in her journal:

> We modeled group conferencing with Denise's story about her visit to
> St. Louis. She had visited St. Louis twice because her grandmothers had
> passed. The children were touched by the remorse of death. This
> extended to a discussion about missing their father's presence in their
> homes. There was some dream and spirit stories told as well. The chil-
> dren are often in the midst of tragic situations involving violent death of
> family members. With the mention of a death often tears well in chil-
> dren's eyes. Some hold their ears in fear of hearing more (ALLEN!).

Many of the children in our class are affected by fears that threaten
to overwhelm and disrupt their learning. They want to confront their fears
but often do not know how. Allen and Nora remind us that writing is a
form of expression, in both a collective and an individual sense, that allows
children a reasonable alternative to "holding their ears" and running away
from their fears. Writing can be an effective way to understand a child's
tears; understanding is critical to the development and growth of our children as human beings and learners.

As Nora's classmates prodded her to think more about the issues surrounding her flashbacks, and as she began to feel comfortable with the
idea of writing as a way of understanding, she began to write in a more
serious fashion. Each day during the first few weeks of November, she
could be seen writing furiously. The next moment Nora would share her
draft and ideas with Alanna, a close and empathetic friend. One morning

in mid-November, Nora had a request. Could she share her new story with the class?

"It is much longer than 'Flashback,'" Nora said.

Softly, just slightly above a whisper, she began to read.

MY FATHER

One night I had a dream about my father getting hurt. It was that he was driving on the freeway when a black Mustang was speeding in a slow lane. My father was getting ready to move into the fast lane. When the black car hit my father and made his car go out of control and hit the freeway wall, I woke up crying.

My father is tall and very big. He used to take me out for dinner and buy me clothes. My relationship with him wasn't very good because my stepfather did not really like how we got along. I'm not mad at my stepfather, but I was my father's first child and I wanted to at least have a good relationship with him.

One night in my basement, two nights after my dream, my mother told me that my father really got killed in a car accident. The accident was on September 1, 1992, the day before she told me. I started to cry and tried to hold it in, but I couldn't. The accident was just like my dream. When they crashed, his head smashed into the compact alarm system in his car. Because my dad is a large size, he had protected two people from going over the seat and through the window. He saved both of their lives.

When I went to his funeral, his eyes looked like it was sewed up and puffy. He had his hair in a ponytail, and it was shiny. I did not want to touch him because the night before I had watched a comedy, "Totally Hidden Video," where the people were at a funeral, and the dead man jumped out of the casket and scared everyone. That's why I was scared to touch him even if he's my dad.

I didn't know anyone at the funeral, but everybody was crying, and it happened to be my relatives. One lady had on an all black dress with a black hat. She was crying hard. She started crying as soon as she saw my dad. My mother and Aunt Sharon, better know as Ronnie, were asking if I had seen that lady before. But I told her "NO" every time she asked me.

After that I met my relatives at the dinner. After I met my relative, I went over to my Aunt Ellen's. Then I went to my Aunt Leana's house. I did not know her well, and I stayed over there five days. They spoiled me, like they took me out for dinner every night. And when I was done, they took me shopping. I love my real relatives because they treat me with respect. They love me, and I love all of them too.

During her reading, Nora paused several times to wipe away tears. It was a difficult few moments for her. Did she really want to share her feelings with the other children? Could they help her understand? Should she have gone beyond her original story?

Later, Nora recalled that moment. "Sometimes you don't even want people to know that [her father's passing], but after a long period of time you might want somebody to know how you feel. It makes you feel better that someone knows—someone cares. So you're willing to take a chance now and share some personal things."

Was Nora thinking about Allen's story as she read? After all, she knew that Allen felt better afterwards and more clearly understood his feelings about the death of his parents. But did she truly understand the risks of sharing?

During another pause in her reading, muffled sounds interrupted the stillness of the classroom. Laughter? The disturbance became indelibly etched in Nora's mind. "Some of them put a book over their face and laughed."

Nora must have suspected at the time that children's tears are not always understood, even by other children. Yet she had some sense of why there appeared to be a lack of empathy among a few of the children. Perhaps they sensed their own fears. "They made fun of me 'cause they never experienced it."

Fortunately, the air of uneasiness that permeated the room during Nora's reading did not discourage her. A greater urge motivated her actions: "It's about my father, and I care about him." Caring, for Nora, meant remembering and expressing herself through writing. From one perspective, we might say that Nora developed and shared her story as a means to an end. It was a personal effort, with personal goals: *she* would feel better and could get on with her life. Yet we know from our experience that stories like these emerge within a social context, as if the writers knew that they could not grow within a social vacuum. We didn't tell Nora that she should write to affect the feelings of others. She wanted to share her experience with other children.

When we peel off another layer in this complex story, the promise of collective growth becomes even more apparent. The day after Nora first read "My Father" to the class, she was approached by Hiram and Aneka. Empathy abounded. At the time, Nora commented, "They have had flashbacks too, and I read my story to them [again] and they understood me. They know and they feel just the same way I do because they've experienced things like that."

Although Hiram and Aneka never wrote about their own fears, we believe that Nora's story rooted itself in the storied memories of both children to emerge at another place and another time.

Just as Allen's story about the death of his parents prompted Nora to write about her own father, so Nora's story about fear and grief motivated Alanna to confront her brother's death. Nine-year-old Alanna, a prolific writer, loved to tell stories and relied on multiple forms of expression to do so. "I can make my stories into song," she once noted. When referring to a photograph that had special meaning for her she said, "Cut me out and put me in the picture."

Alanna knew the value of a good story, but not until she started meeting with Nora, after the reading of "My Father," was she able to admit that there was one story she had not been able to tell. Alanna confided in Nora that her older brother died in an auto accident when she was six, and although she wanted to remember him, she had a difficult time doing so. Nora remembered their first meetings. "After she read 'My Father,' she felt that she should write about her brother. It helped her to get it out because she usually cries and everything about it."

After hearing about Nora's father Alanna told Nora that she missed her brother very much and wanted to remember again. Alanna began two stories in which her love and her grief for her brother slowly emerged. First she wrote "When I Go Fishing," a heartwarming story about a brother she loved, who protected her, and who, like her, loved to fish. Then she wrote a more definitive story, "My Brother Joel," in which she came to terms with her fears about her brother's death. She wrote, "I thought I had to get another brother, and my mother laughed. She said, 'He will always be your brother in spirit.'"

We have learned much from observing Nora, Allen, and Alanna. Telling their stories allowed them to experience hope in the face of tragedy. After writing about her brother, Alanna commented that she felt good because "I can remember him." But the overriding value of these stories is that they give children a chance to confront their fears and share with others who might help them understand.

⊡⊡⊡

Recently, Rhonda, a young girl in our class, stepped timidly to the front of the room to read a story she had just written about her cat. She told about her love for her cat, her attempts to save him during his illness, and her moment of reflection as she laid him to rest in the ground behind her garage. As she finished her reading, Tamara raised her hand to ask why she wrote such a story. Rhonda paused and then gave a meek but firm reply: "[Writing] gets the sadness down on paper," said Rhonda. "When I write it down I get the sadness out." And others, we might add, become participants in the encounter with one of life's more frightening mysteries.

Paul; One Writer's Emergence

Silhouetted in the morning light that filtered in through an uncurtained window, Paul sat with Dan at a single computer located next to Vicki's desk. A telephone line linked the computer to the Internet, providing the class with access to e-mail. Convinced that he needed an expert on African American history to answer his questions, Paul had decided to write to the director of African American studies at a nearby university. Paul thought his words out carefully as he dictated them to Dan.

> My name is Paul Strayer. I am in the fourth grade. I want to know a lot about slavery. It's part of me. I want to know. I wonder if my mom and

grandmom had to live that way, in the bad scenes of police on them. I hope that you can tell me a lot about slavery, because I would like to know. Thank you for helping me out. I will write about what you tell me and what I know. Paul Strayer.

The director understood Paul's urgency. Two days later he responded with an invitation: "Would you like to visit our university and tour the Center for African American Studies?" Paul accepted, and one week later a small group of students and teachers paid a visit to the center. It was an auspicious day, especially for Paul. As we listened to him talk with the director, we were captivated by the complexity of the questions implicit in his statements.

"Back then they was slaves, but then, like, in the sixties . . . when they met Dr. Martin Luther King . . . they [whites] was like . . . Dr. Martin Luther King was showing them the right way, and they didn't like it. So they tried to do *everything* they could to get them away from Dr. Martin Luther King. Like, if they see somebody drinking out of the good water fountains, they would arrest them for nothing."

Paul returned from that spring visit in 1990 excited and confident about his writing. Eight months earlier, in the fall of 1989, we knew a different, less confident Paul. Reading and writing were incidental to his other classroom activities: talking, daydreaming, and drawing pictures in his notebook. Writing was difficult. His frequent starts and stops frustrated him and perplexed us. Reading found him going through the motions of holding a book as if to read a story, when in fact he saw only strings of letters instead of recognizable words. He appeared hopelessly behind in the most basic reading and writing skills. Yet his oral skills were well honed. He readily joined in conversation with the other children when class time allowed for a more personal response to complex topics.

Within our first few weeks of knowing Paul we concluded that we needed a specific teaching strategy to enhance his language skills. Rather than label him as yet another student hopelessly lost in the system, we put his weaknesses as a literacy learner into perspective. From the beginning of the school year, we noted several positive signs that identified Paul as an experienced thinker: his willingness to discuss complex issues and his enthusiasm for ideas. He was not really lost. He was merely waiting for an invitation to join in the learning community, an invitation that made sense, and one he could confidently accept. What Paul needed was access to a process that could offer him an open door for his imagination.

Paul's grandmother noted that he had entered fourth grade with many deficiencies as a writer and reader. "He only went to school about a third of the time for his first three years, and his life at home was not stable. He was passed on by the school system."

Three years of social promotion had left Paul stumbling over the words in most picture books. His writing had not developed beyond that of a typical emergent writer several years younger than he. During those first three grades, when Paul attended school less than part of the time, he was lost in an educational system of 170,000 students. Yet despite the educational setbacks he had suffered, he was bursting with ideas, framed mostly in the stories he told his classmates. At first he told stories because he wanted to be noticed in class. Any story would do as long as someone was listening and he was the center of attention. But during our first "Neighborhood Tour" (an event originated and organized by the children to share their community with guest teachers), Paul's focus as a storyteller changed. He began to express himself in relation to a more complex world.

On a cool and windy October morning, thirty-five children guided three teachers on a tour of their neighborhood. Blocks of neighborhood homes and small businesses shared one-lane alleys, each block sectioned by intersecting streets to form a typical city grid. At one point in the tour, the children stopped to mingle noisily near a rusted cyclone fence that surrounded a neighborhood playground.

Dan's video camera captured Shaleena as she spoke above the din of voices. "In the summer, they got a program up here where they play games and stuff, and they have lunch at this park."

"My auntie, she work at the recreation center . . . Sometimes I go with her," James added in support.

Paul interrupted. "It used to be—a long time ago—people used to be fightin' and shootin' and all that stuff. Beatin' people up, and dogs came around."

"You used to go there a lot?" asked Vicki.

"I used to go there mostly every day, but now I stopped 'cause they be fightin' and shootin' and stuff. And the dogs be coming out and bitin' people." His voice trailed off as he turned to follow the crowd of children already moving on to the next familiar landmark.

After the tour, when we had returned to the classroom, Paul joined in the general class discussion and resumed his talk about the park. He expressed resentment that he was unable visit his former playground and he described his weekly bus trips to a less convenient but safer park a few miles from his home. Other children played off Paul's comments about neighborhood conditions. One group described a cinder-block building known as the Motor Cycle Club. Tyra gestured to a garage with white and black trim that she had helped her father paint. Still another child found it unbelievable that a local gang allegedly burnt down his favorite Burger King. On camera we had recorded the Burger King building: plywood windows and a charred brick wall, which contrasted starkly with the hand-painted sign covering a window: "CLOSED."

When the bell ended our discussion, the students exited noisily. We were left exhausted but energized by their enthusiasm. How could we capture this kind of excitement in our writing workshops every day? Our students routinely fought us over writing and asking endless questions: "What can I write about? How do you spell . . . ? How long does it have to be?" But having witnessed the dynamic involvement of Paul and the other children in the tour, we began to rethink our motives. When the children described themselves within the context of their own neighborhood, they not only exuded confidence, they displayed impressive knowledge.

The tour proved pivotal in the development of our writing workshops, but it was most noteworthy for Paul, who had so often been labeled a "reluctant writer." The next day, we asked the children to compile a list of neighborhood-related topics they might write about. Paul's list was short, yet focused: more than anything else, he wanted to write about the park. Looking back, we realize that he was about to embark on an odyssey that affected him and many of those he encountered during that notable year. It was an odyssey shaped by his own process of writing, and one which allowed him to make sense of the complex world in which he lived.

After several weeks of writing, erasing, conferring, and checking spellings with his peers, Paul set his essay "The Park" on Vicki's desk. "Finished," said Paul.

There was a park the place for boys and gils to play. But ther [referring to gangs] going, smoking pot. So then the kids stop come to the park . . . The police come to look out so the park can stay clean. But the park never stay clean. The kids like me and you can't go to the park. This is not fair to the kids like me. I hope this will stop soon.

It was a powerful story all by itself. But we knew Paul had more to tell. He had often talked about the park with his classmates during conferences. He was not shy about discussing it. But he needed more practice in writing to be able to handle his complex ideas. We understood that he struggled as a writer, but we wanted push him as well. Too much of Paul's life story was being lost to him in the confusion of informal conversations. We asked him to read the piece to the class, hoping that other children would persuade him to develop it further. We were willing to allow him the whole school year if necessary to finish at least one good piece for his writing folder, which up until December remained empty.

Initial class reaction to "The Park" was encouraging. Other students agreed with Paul that the old, warm and inviting neighborhood park had become a more ominous place. But they also had questions. "Why did you say that? What about the gangs? Where will we play now? How come you said, 'ther going, smoking pot'?" Paul was confused. Hadn't he answered these questions in his story?

We understood his confusion. He knew what he meant in "The Park," but he couldn't see that his words conveyed only part of his meaning to his audience. Paul's responses to the students' questions were vague, and in the end, as we should have expected considering his past frustrations with writing, he decided that "The Park" was finished. Although he spent several more days talking about it with some of his classmates, soon after he filed it in his writing folder without revisions.

On the surface, Paul had given us an answer to a question we had raised earlier. When he spoke, he was confident. In talking with his peers, he was able to interweave their comments and his own to form a well-developed argument. We could not say the same about his writing. Throughout the first four months of the school year, it was scant in quantity and not fully developed. His unfinished writing folder held a collection of wandering fragments that seemed to settle like fallout on the page. He wrote haphazardly, here about gangs and violence, there about child safety in the city. In a story he named "The Gas Station," Paul wrote several sentences but crossed out all but two. These at least could have become the framework for a paragraph:

There was a gas station . . . [undecipherable words]. They are fixing it up.

As of January, however, "The Park" remained the only finished story in which Paul attempted to go beyond his topic idea.

It was a frustrating time. Paul seemed sincere about wanting to write, but his completed work seemed to belie his sincerity. For a couple of weeks we were at a standstill. We cajoled; he stiffened. We implored; he went through the motions of writing. Paul did not give up on writing. It was just that writing was not the easiest way for him to understand and express his thoughts on complex issues. He was moving ahead cautiously. In terms of his skills, he was still an emerging writer, and no one had ever asked him to write about things that interested him before. He sensed that writing could be as effective as his spoken narratives were, and in his own way, he continued to sift through the ideas that played in his mind.

Several days after our neighborhood tour and visit to the park, Paul questioned Aimee, his grandmother, "Why wasn't it safe to go there anymore?" Accustomed to Paul's inquisitiveness and his concern about the community, she responded with a story. "My Aunt Kate, that I would stay with during the summer, lived on Afra street near John R. During that time it was nicer in the area. We used to go to the Fox Theatre, two, three, four movies in one day. We'd play in the street, I can remember, with Martha Reeves and the Vandellas. We'd block off the street. We was right there, my sisters and I, with Martha. We started dancing in the street, and she went back and wrote the song 'Dancing in the Street.'" Softly, she began to sing: "Don't forget the Motor City. All we need is music, sweet music. There'll be music everywhere . . ."

"I can remember Diana Ross living in the Brewster Projects. I knew when she lived there. I remember them all. We was right in that group, 'cause Afra and John R. is right in between the Brewster Projects and Woodward Avenue. And they kept the fruit stand on corners where you could buy hot tamales and fruit. It would be real hot in the apartment building. My aunt and the older people would sit out on the porch, on the steps of the apartment building. She would allow us to walk up to the corner, which was a block and a half away, to buy hot tamales, fruit, or popcorn. And you would be safe! There was no fear there like there is now."

"You were a little girl walking up the street by yourself?"

"Yes. It was safe then. You know it wasn't that people was doing harm to small children and killing, and things like that."

Aimee left Paul with his thoughts. It wasn't until much later in the fall that Vicki found out about Paul's persistence and Aimee's contribution to his understanding. Behind the scenes, outside of school, he barraged his grandmother with questions. In the process, they often spoke of freedom. Paul also became interested in news reports that Nelson Mandela had been released from prison.

"I want to know why people be treated that way." Paul said to his grandmother. "Why did they have to come from the other side [Africa]? They didn't harm the other people, so why should they harm the black people?"

According to his grandmother, Paul's questions were part of a larger search he had carried out over the years, ever since he first saw a picture of her great grandfather. "The picture would be right on the mantel. And he wanted to know 'Who is that old man and lady?' And I told him who he was. My great grandfather, an ex-slave. He told us stories, and I told Paul. I can remember him saying that 'they line you up and they'll say, I'll take that one. The most healthy one. And I'll take that one and this one.' And my great grandfather said he was just hoping that they wouldn't take him, 'cause he wanted to stay with his family. But they chose him. He didn't know his real, biological family."

For Paul, the issue of slavery and freedom had complicated his family's life for a long time. In retrospect, it is not difficult to see why he had difficulty writing about the park. It was one small piece of the freedom puzzle that dominated his thinking.

Paul finally found his voice as a writer in late spring, at the time he made his visit to the director of the African American studies program. Paul's positive relationship with the director seems to have been critical in his decision to write about freedom. By connecting past and present in the lives of African Americans, the director rekindled Paul's thinking about other forms of oppression among blacks. Soon after, Vicki noted in her journal:

> Paul and Michael conferred in the corridor—giving them space and privacy. When I checked on them, it looked as if they were writing Paul's story as a team. As they talked, Paul wrote while Michael spelled for him. . . . Paul was writing on being enslaved by drugs. He felt that you haven't a mind of your own. "Drugs dictate to you—they lead your life!" he said. Paul is a thinker and expresses himself well. He has worked with several students recently, often selecting the person who he sees as serious for the day.

In later interviews with Paul, we discovered that his visit to the university had reinforced ideas that had been with him for the greater part of his short life. He talked about his mother's devastating experience with drugs and about how his own uncle's drug habit was a form of slavery. "She [Aunt] was telling me how it could take over your life. You would give anything to get it. My uncle—he did it! He did anything to get him some—just go around the corner and get some drugs."

Within two weeks of his university visit, Paul submitted the draft of a story to a committee of children responsible for organizing and editing a collection of children's writings. Several days later he read his completed story to the class.

ENSLAVED

Slavery was unfair because they was beaten and taken from their family. And I bet that the hardest part is to be taken away from your family because they took care of you since you was born. And most of the white people did not care about how the slaves felt. Those white people was too lazy and they wanted to take the slaves from their home in Africa.

All the slaves was on a ship. The ship was no bigger than the classroom. The slaves was dying because if somebody got sick then the others will get sick and they will die too. When they made it to the south there was to sign a contract to do service for twenty years, but they got tricked to serve for life! I don't think that is fair, do you? But that's how it was.

Now, I want to tell you about Nelson Mandella. He was a leader in Africa. He showed them the right way for a long time. Then he went to court and lost the case and he was in jail for twenty-seven years. He's out now in 1990. He is all around the world. I'm glad he's out to turn the idea of Black's getting along with Whites the right way.

Now I want to tell you about Harriet Tubman. I learned this in a book and in a story that my teacher read to our class. Harriet was a slave since she was 4 years old. She had to take care of one, two, and three year olds when she was only four or five years old herself. And if she didn't do right she will get beaten with a belt or whip. When she got older she would get locked in a box for a lot of hours or for a day. I know Harriet was treated bad but the White people didn't have no feeling for slaves. All they wanted was there house to get cleaned and some of the slaves didn't know how to read. Some of the slaves had to sneak to learn to read.

Back to the story. The part I didn't like was when she had got hit in the head with a weight. She was out for a week then she was not feeling right. Nobody wanted her but she started the underground railroad. She

made it to the free side but she was not happy because she was thinking about her family. She went back to the South to free her family.
She tricked everybody on the south side and they wanted her head
dead or alive, but they can't not find her but her and her family was
free.

> But you are still a slave to drugs because drugs can make you a
slave. Say like I was on drugs I will be a slave. Because drugs is telling me
what to do. Drugs can be harmful. There are steroids, crack, pot, weed,
alcohol, and cigarette. Back to the point how drugs can effect your life.
They can kill you, in a day, or probably a week. I don't see why people do
drugs. It's killing our city. People killing each other over crack. You are an
addict to crack. You are robbing and killing, smoking, and dealing. Crack is
stupid. But people think it is fun, and they get high off it. It's making people
go and kill other people. Because drugs is telling them what to do. I hope
that the world will stop killing because I don't want my family to get killed
over drugs. Because I will die before my family.

As we consider the paths Paul took as a writer in our class, we recognize our own naiveté. Our invitation to write at the beginning of the school
year was a bit ill-conceived. Asking a student to write and providing a
physical space in the classroom is not enough. Children need many spaces
and many kinds of invitations in order to engage in the process we call
writing. They need to be allowed to make sense of an idea that they might
eventually write about. Paul, for instance, needed to explore his own home
and neighborhood, and talk to other people before he could write about
a topic that meant so much to him.

In June, Paul sat proudly on a six-by-eight-foot carpet remnant
between two bookshelves in the back of the room, a meeting place the
children called "The Writers' Café." In a quiet voice, eyes shifting
between us and the view outside the window, Paul spoke about his experiences as a writer in general, and as the author of "Enslaved" in particular:
"Before, I never thought about writing what happened to me. I would tell
about it, like in a story, but I would never have dreamed about writing it
on a piece of paper. I never thought I would be a writer. I knew I could
copy something down and write it really good. I could write up on the
board. I could write what the teacher writes about. When people tell me
something, I can write about it and that changes me. *You* give yourself
ideas and not the teacher!"

In reviewing our first impressions of Paul and his reluctance to write, we understand that he never really lost sight of his desire to inform others about the way things were in his life: he was prohibited from playing in the neighborhood park because of circumstances over which he had very little control. If we did anything for Paul it is that we created a space for him to explore what it means to be a writer and a literacy learner.

Rebecca: Eulogy for a Grandfather

The hallway emptied of children. By the time everyone else had retreated behind the closing doors of classrooms, Rebecca stood alone with Vicki. Quietly, she whispered, "Mrs. Rybicki, my grandma said to tell you that my granddaddy passed last night."

Vicki's face flushed. She had blanked on Rebecca's name.

"Sweetheart, had he been real sick?"

"My grandma said that he just slipped away."

Vicki gently put her arm around Rebecca and held her close. Rebecca had been in Vicki's homeroom for two years, as a third and fourth grader. Her elderly grandfather and grandmother were caring for her at the time. She liked to tell stories about her grandfather, who was impatient, sick—and very close to her. Vicki looked at Rebecca.

"How about if you come to my classroom after school today? I'll take you home and visit with your grandma."

Rebecca nodded and walked across the hall to her fifth-grade classroom. Still reflecting on Rebecca and her loss, Vicki closed the door to her classroom and began directing her students to their desks. She wondered, *Would Rebecca return this afternoon?* Images flooded her mind as she recalled the African American tradition of mourning. She remembered when Jamie died in a house fire, and when Terry Spaulding was killed. Then there was Charlotte's husband, who died after a bout with cancer. It was customary in African American families not to schedule funeral home visits. Instead their houses were filled with people singing, hugging, eating. The richness and power of death's "transition," its grieving and its talking in celebrating "a life," take time, often a week or more. The home of the bereaved draws family, friends, and ministers. Relatives and friends double their work shifts to allow for the long and tiring hours they drive to comfort the bereaved.

Marcus interrupted Vicki's thoughts. "Mrs. Rybicki, on the playground this morning . . . " The noise of children at their desks brought her back to the classroom, and she settled in to a morning of teaching.

After school, Rebecca arrived promptly at Vicki's door. She was excited. She had seen other children getting a ride home from Vicki before and secretly desired the privilege. In the car, she sat up proudly and waved to the children mingling in front of school, yet she was reluctant to enter into conversation. As Vicki parked the car, Rebecca stretched her body half out of the seat to see who was at the house. Graciously, Rebecca's auntie greeted both of them at the door and welcomed them quickly inside. An uncle hugged Rebecca and a distant aunt helped her with her schoolbag. Then Rebecca and her auntie quietly disappeared into a bedroom. Comforting voices and inviting spirituals from a nearby room interrupted Vicki's thoughts. Attracted to the sounds, Vicki entered the tightly packed dining room to curious, but polite stares and the tantalizing smell of fried chicken. A few friends and relatives engaged in quiet conversation as they played cards. Most of the people in the room looked up and smiled when Vicki was introduced. There was talk of all kinds: small talk, polite talk, cautious talk, friendly talk.

"Mrs. Rybicki [mispronouncing as Rybacki], Rebecca's granddad had a peaceful transition. We were blessed. Etta [Rebecca's grandmother] is making arrangements at the funeral home . . . Rebecca'll bring the information to school tomorrow."

Slightly bent in her chair, an elderly woman sitting next to Vicki closed her eyes and began to hum softly. Her body expressed the sense of mourning everyone seemed to feel.

Steal away
Steal away
Steal away to Jesus
Steal away
Steal away home
I ain't got long to stay here.

My lord he calls me
He calls me by the thunder
the trumpet sounds within my soul
I ain't got long to stay here.

"Won't you rest your coat, Mrs. Rybicki? Etta will be back soon." Vicki explained that her visit was intended to be short, and that she would return to pay her respects at a later time.

Rebecca's auntie escorted Vicki to the car.

"I'll bring a dish tomorrow," said Vicki.

"Oh yes! That would be most appreciated . . . Mrs. Nesbitt will be happy to know that you stopped by."

As Vicki drove away, she thought about her return to Rebecca's home in a few days. How could she comfort Rebecca? That evening, Vicki began to search through Rebecca's writing folders and found a couple of stories about her grandfather. In the morning, before school started, Vicki pored over Rebecca's files. She found more stories, some complete and some unfinished, and reflections in her journal about her grandfather. Slowly, as she began to grasp the full extent of Rebecca's writing about her grandfather, Vicki sank back in her chair. Piece by piece, Rebecca had assembled a complex story about her relationship with her grandfather. No wonder she had shared her grief with Vicki. It was in Vicki's classroom over a two-year period that Rebecca had learned to trust her classmates and her teacher, who encouraged her in her loving relationship with her grandfather.

With these samples of Rebecca's writing scattered before her, Vicki began to trace the pattern of Rebecca's thinking. At the beginning of third grade, Rebecca wrote about the book *Sweet Valley Kids*, focusing almost exclusively on one character's birthday. Then, as if reminded, she finished up with an emphatic "Today is my grandfather's birthday."

Vicki paused to take in the full meaning of grandparents in the lives of her students. In many homes an aged and/or afflicted grandmother governs the house from her bed on the living room sofa. More than a third of the children who attend this neighborhood school are being raised by their grandparents or live with a parent in their grandparents' home, and many spend their infancy and first years there. This care-giving clearly fosters deeply rooted relationships with grandparents.

For Vicki, reinforcing the importance of the elderly, especially grandparents, in the lives of children was nothing new. Books such as *When I Am Old with You*, *The Wednesday Surprise*, *Halmoni and the Picnic*, *Grandfather Bill's Story*, and *The Hundred Penny Box* line the shelves of her classroom, and children read and talk about them often. In fact, Vicki had read *The Hundred Penny Box* aloud to Rebecca and her classmates over several weeks during the winter of Rebecca's third-grade year. Michael, a principal character in the book, ponders the storytelling and singing of his great-aunt Dew. A family treasure, she is an important part of Michael's home life. Michael has deep respect for his great-aunt. He loves her slow, throaty harmonizing in the gospel song "Precious Lord."

The children loved the book, Michael, and one-hundred-year-old Aunt Dew, and identified with the characters. This was especially true of Rebecca, who was writing her own story about an elderly family member she loved, her grandfather.

USE YOUR HEND FOR MORE THEN A HAT RAKIT

When I was two my grandfather he still say it, "Use your head for more then a hat rakit," but I ask him "What does that mean?" he say "that is a old saying." then I But "What does that mean?" Mrs. Rybicki fanaly told me what does that mean. "It mean to use your brain instad of puting brow rats in it."

In recalling this moment, Vicki realized that Rebecca was, for the first time, acknowledging the importance of her grandfather and the stories he told. For the most part, however, her efforts to write about her grandfather showed up in her Reflection Journal. In one of her last entries that year, she wrote about *The Lucky Stone*.

This book remind me when my grandfather, when he would tell one of his long old story about when he was a boy in west virginia.

The next fall, as a new fourth grader in Vicki's language arts class, Rebecca picked up where she had left off. In fact, her passion to talk and write about her grandfather increased by the week. Vicki recalled the time Rebecca read aloud her reflections about the book *Children of Long Ago*.

I really like this page . . . a poem about reading glasses. It makes me think about my grandpa. I'm going home to my grandpa "Can you read this book to me please? Like I used to do when I was little?" [Rebecca talks about the new book.] It made me feel so good.

Several children raised their hands.

"Tameka," said Rebecca.

"Why do you like your grandpa reading to you?"

Rebecca fielded this and a dozen similar questions about grandparents and their relationships with children. She was thrilled with the class response.

A few weeks later, Rebecca revisited *The Hundred Penny Box* and wrote in her Reflection Journal.

ARE YOUR ARMS HUNDRED YEARS OLD?

I thought I was in the story. Michael really did care about Aunt Dew. I thought I was in the story My grandpa is just like Aunt Dew. for a minute, I was Michael . . . Yesterday it was my grandpa's birthday hes 80, but hes not old as Aunt Dew.

Vicki stared at the journal entry. Rebecca had drawn an arrow from this entry on the left-hand page to the facing page, where another entry lay unfinished.

"The reason I say my granpa tells stories like Aunt Dew . . ."

For Vicki it was a moment of discovery. She remembered how, when Rebecca began to reread *The Hundred Penny Box*, she had engaged in several conversations about grandparents. The unfinished entry was apparently an attempt to make explicit the connections Rebecca had been making herself for a long time: the stories she read about the elderly and those she wrote and told about her grandfather were connected. It occurred to Vicki that almost any story could serve as a way for Rebecca to talk about the grandfather she loved so much.

Rebecca's second reading of *The Hundred Penny Box* motivated her to write a story. At the time, her grandfather had become ill, and nine-year-old Rebecca was frantic with worry. She could not separate her experiences at school from her experiences at home, nor did she see a need to. Several weeks later, Rebecca submitted the draft of a new story to a small group discussion.

MY GRANDFATHER'S STORY

One Sunday night my grandfather was telling me a story. That night he told me about my uncle William when he was my age. He said when my uncle William was my age, that's nine, he said there were only three kids in the whole neighborhood his age and that was William and his two twin friends Jim and Tim.

They came in the house to get something to drink. My grandfather started the story over and over again and he finally got to the point. "That was when black and white TV's were out," he said.

Then the twin, Jim came in and started watching TV and it turned pitch black. Then Jim said, "Ooh, it's dark. I got to get home." The door was wide open and it was daylight.

When my grandfather finished his story, he got so happy he yelled, "It is dark." My aunt jumped straight up in the bed out of her sleep.

My Uncle William said, "Man how dumb can you get."

They teased Jim until it wasn't funny anymore.

During the discussion, Rebecca revealed important connections to her story. On a significant scale, it celebrates her grandfather's humor before his illness. When he told stories to family members, he would become excited and blurt out the punch line: "Man how dumb can you get." The loud laughter that followed woke Rebecca's aunt, napping in a nearby room.

Vicki remembered when Rebecca shared the scene. It was all so funny, and the other children joined in the laughter. But humor was only part of it. Rebecca's story also shows what a special person her grandfather was to her. He was *the* family storyteller, and his stories were treasured by family members, especially his granddaughter. His storytelling was an important social act: it reinforced his closeness to Rebecca as he told stories and her affection for him as she listened.

After she had introduced "My Grandfather's Story" to the whole class, Rebecca talked about him further in smaller peer groups. Her classmates challenged her to continue working on "My Grandfather's Story" and to develop other stories about her grandfather that "make you feel good." Rebecca responded by writing several new stories, each of which gave her another opportunity to talk about her grandfather.

In January she wrote "My Life Flashed Before My Eyes," a story celebrating her grandfather's courage during a neighborhood blackout. In confusion, Rebecca and other family members ran to the basement, but when she looked around the dimly lit room she noticed that her grandfather was missing. Bravely, she sneaked upstairs. Her grandfather had found the cause of the blackout, but with it, a new danger.

> He looked out the window and a wire had fallen. It was a wierd sound and we went outside. I was scared.

Amid the confusion of the blackout, the neighbors had and retreated to the street, a safe distance from their homes and any potential fire. But just as the last of them reached the street, Rebecca's grandfather returned to his house. Rebecca panicked.

> I went back in the house and told my grandfather to get out of the house, but he said, "I'm not going anywhere." So I went back outside. I was sad because he could have died.

Vicki pulled "The Tooth Fairy" from Rebecca's writing folder, a story about her discovery of the tooth fairy myth. She had wondered if the tooth fairy was real.

> But my Grandaddy said, "No," putting his hand on his face and shaking his head meaning no. "It's just an old saying."

In the spring, Rebecca began to read *The Front Porch Stories*, about a father's storytelling. Time and again, until school let out for the year,

Rebecca returned to this book. It was known affectionately as "Rebecca's book." Although Rebecca was supposed to return it to the book corner at the back of the room each day, she chose to keep it under her desk, just in case.

Moving scattered papers aside, Vicki reached for a copy of the book. What was it that Rebecca valued about it so much? The cover showed a father and his two daughters sitting on the front stoop. Both daughters are leaning forward, lovingly resting their arms on his leg. Their eyes connect. A friendly rag fire, used to ward off mosquitoes on a warm summer night, glows in an old washtub at the base of the stoop. In the firelight, ominous shadows flicker on the steps behind the trio—an ideal setting for telling good stories.

Vicki imagined Rebecca reading *The Front Porch Stories* and sensing in the love and closeness between this storyteller and his listeners her own historical, cultural, and family connections. In the author's memories of her childhood, where stories played such an important role, Rebecca saw similarities to her own life. This notion became clearer to Vicki when she read one of the final entries in Rebecca's Reflection Journal. Margie and Ethel, the sisters in the book, were fascinated by their father's stories. Rebecca wrote,

> Margie and Ethel are asking questions about the story he have told them. One of the Question were What was the shadow . . . Everyone left Margie on the Porch. She got scared. She thought the headlight of a truck was Grandpa Wally's ghost.

When she compared the original story, Vicki realized that Rebecca's version was somewhat inaccurate. Rebecca, for example, thinks the headlight is on a truck, but in the story it is a lantern on a barge in the river. Rebecca's interpretation seems odd unless we view it as an important reader response: the truck light makes more sense to her than a river barge lantern. And it is not difficult to imagine that she was influenced by the fact that Margie and Ethel's dad told stories that had been passed down from Grandpa Wally, the family storyteller. In the book, Grandpa Wally appears only in passing, in the father's conversations with his daughters; it is the father who is the storyteller and main character. In Rebecca's version, however, it is the grandfather.

Vicki was not surprised by Rebecca's year-end literacy activities. As she gathered up the various papers and folders, she thought, *Stories stay with Rebecca and serve as ways to hold on to pleasant memories.*

The day before the funeral, Rebecca stopped by Vicki's classroom to give her a program for the service. Vicki hugged her. As she turned to go, Vicki's words followed her. "I have something for you, Rebecca. It's your story about your grandfather. I thought you might find comfort in it at this time. I'll stop by your house tomorrow."

On the morning of the funeral, Vicki arrived at Rebecca's house before school with a tray of hot chicken wings—and her apologies. The administration would not allow her to miss school to attend the service for Rebecca's grandfather and guardian.

"I should have insisted that someone attend. I'll stop by again during my prep period."

Later in the morning, Vicki slipped away from school unnoticed to pay her respects to Rebecca and her family. At the funeral home, Rebecca's grandmother greeted Vicki and led her to the minister's car, where Rebecca sat in the front passenger's seat. Vicki gave Rebecca a hug and a kiss, adding that she would pray.

"I love you Rebecca," Vicki whispered.

The minister turned in her direction but made no comment. Just then the funeral director motioned for Vicki to move her car in line just behind the family's car.

Embarrassed, Vicki moved her lips and motioned with her hands to say, "No—school!" Slowly and sadly, she drove away.

The following week, Rebecca told Vicki that her grandmother had asked an aunt to read her story at the funeral. Although other relatives protested, not understanding how Rebecca's story fit in with the other eulogies, her grandmother insisted. She had also come to realize what the "My Grandfather's Story" meant to Rebecca. It was her legacy from her grandfather, rich with reminders of her relationship with him.

Gathering Rebecca in her arms, Vicki spoke words heard often in her classroom as she responded to the children: "I know how important that story is to you . . ."

Allen: Product of the Environment

The city will try to stop the custom of firing guns in the air to celebrate New Year's Day . . . "When bullets go up, they've got to come down. And one could go into a window as we saw here . . ."

The police chief pledged to appeal to the "conscience of the people" to stop the practice . . . and to [mount] a campaign similar to the one used to reduce Devil's Night fires. (*The Blade*, January 1996)

The local news story struck us forcefully. We were nearing the end of the 1995–96 winter break, a time we had set aside to complete this book about the effects of children's life stories on their writing. Random gunfire on New Year's Eve was an escalating problem, according the police chief, and this time a forty-nine-year-old woman had been shot and killed. We found it ironic that this story appeared just as we were writing about Allen, a child in our class who, six years earlier, had written about guns and violence in the city. Like Allen, the police chief also pleaded for action.

From our experience, we knew that random acts of violence during times of community celebration disturbed our students. We thought back to the Devil's Night initiative of 1990 in the city where Vicki teaches, which drew local and national media coverage. Thirty thousand community activists formed a coalition to reduce fires and crime significantly on the nights preceding Halloween. We remembered our noisy classroom discussion about the event. To a passerby listening from the hallway, the loud voices coming from our room that day could have been mistaken for an off-key chorus rehearsal. But to us it seemed that the children had merely forgotten Robert's Rules of Order. Passion ruled. Worried children tried to imagine the confusion that would result from the arsonists' actions. Would some of the abandoned houses near the school be set afire? Allen was among those who protested most loudly.

Several months later, Allen brought another important community problem to the class's attention—gunfire as an expression of celebration. They all knew of relatives who fired gunshots in the air on New Year's Eve, and Allen had begun to write about the issue.

"The police got to have guns," Allen explained to the class. But in the same breath he added, "Is it OK to have guns?"

Allen and the other students were confused. There was disagreement. As we listened to the children, we noted that the issue was not one a child, or an adult for that matter, could fully understand in one brief discussion. When the children asked Allen for more, it marked the beginning of Allen's emergence as a serious writer in our classroom.

From his first day as a fourth grader, Allen stood out. According to previous teachers and counselors he was streetwise and often truant. He had difficulty with reading and writing and had been held back twice before fourth grade. But the younger children looked up to him as an experienced leader, and he had a natural way of talking to others. In the first few weeks of school, when Allen decided to attend Vicki's language arts class, he expressed his opinions about everything that was brought up in class. He craved public attention, sometimes to the point of being rude. But as the year progressed, we began to notice a subtle change in Allen's classroom behavior. During the time of the Devil's Night initiative, Vicki was writing, "Allen has a tendency to impatiently blurt out his answers. Yet he occasionally cuffs his mouth in respect for another child talking. Allen's probing questions stimulated good class discussions."

Allen was poised from the first day of class to challenge us in a number of rewarding as well as stressful ways. He was a child of contrasts, and loaded with energy. Throughout the early fall, Allen would surprise us with reflective moments alone and with his peers. On the flip side, however, he skipped school often and missed assignments in chunks. By December Allen's name appeared regularly in Vicki's e-mail notes to Dan.

> Allen came to school on a snowy day! He and James were writing and working together quite seriously . . . These two STAY troublesome so it was most interesting to hear them evaluate the process of today's Author's Chair session.

On another occasion in early January, Vicki wrote:

> Wait until you see Allen's new "Do." He has an odd patch of blond hair near his left temple . . . the patch looks as if his skin has been bleached . . . we refused to let this distract us from our study.

We were drawn to Allen's enthusiasm for life, but his inconsistencies as a student learner worried us. One freezing February afternoon, as Vicki and her husband Paul drove away from the school, they noticed two former students fighting on the sidewalk. Allen, who had missed school that day, was standing back, like a cornerman at ringside, holding the hat of one of the fighters. As Paul braked to a stop, everyone scattered except Allen. When Vicki approached him, he sheepishly agreed to accept a ride home.

With a nervous laugh, Allen introduced Vicki to his custodial aunt. "I'm embarrassed that he skipped out," she said. Vicki spoke little about the fight, but she was emphatic about Allen's truancy problem and how it was interfering with his schoolwork. She vowed to find a way to help Allen strengthen his commitment not only to school but to his own learning. When he yelled down the street to a couple of friends, the two women's eyes met in agreement. Allen needed some extra guidance.

Vicki and Paul drove off, mulling strategies that might help Allen. The problems were apparent. Vicki knew that Allen was not too motivated to find interesting topics for reading or writing, and that many of these problems were a result of his lack of reading and writing skills. Yet he was motivated to talk about current issues, especially about violence and guns. There was the time during the Devil's Night discussion when he argued passionately; and there was the time a few days after New Year's Eve.

The fight had an awakening effect on Vicki and Dan. Allen seemed to be serving notice that, in terms of school it was now or never. The day after the fight, Vicki arrived early and sorted through Allen's writing folder, which contained pages of fragmented stories about basketball, friends, and school. There was also the beginning of a story, "Guns," that he had just begun to write and talk about a few days before the fight. We plotted. The issue of guns fascinated Allen. Why not nudge him to develop his story further? We thought it might be the push he needed.

Later that morning, Allen and Dan retreated to the carpeted comfort of "The Writers' Café" to talk about "Guns." Dan asked Allen why the story was important to him.

"I hear about it," Allen said, "on the news! . . . sometimes 'round the corner, like on Jerrod's street." He paused. "Drug dealers. Every time I hear someone is shot—on the news—I think about my story. Should I write that in my story? Should I write this body got killed?"

As Allen spoke, Dan listened attentively. There was a sincerity, an urgency, in Allen's voice that was missing from the written version of his story. Dan was a captive audience, but he wondered about the audience for the written version. "Allen, what would your readers get from your story?"

"If a police officer reads it I think they'll say that this is a good story. I want him to come to us and tell us what should we do. Is it all right to have guns?" Allen's voice trailed off. He had hardly looked at the writing he held in his hands, yet Dan was encouraged and sensed where Allen wanted to go with the story. "Maybe you could write about what you just told me?"

Allen nodded tentatively and headed back to his desk. He didn't do much writing that morning, but he did talk loudly and emphatically about his newfound topic. During lunch, Dan described the interview to Vicki. "The real story was developing nicely in his mind."

"Yes, but it will be much harder for him to develop the same story in written form," Vicki replied. "He is like several others who hesitate to read their writing because some of the words they've used are not spelled correctly, even though they know what the word is and are able to read it. The same phenomenon is what inhibits their writing in the first place."

Despite the apparent difficulties in getting Allen to move beyond his writing errors, we were encouraged by his attempts to expand his original story on guns. He spent most of March revising several key sentences about who needed guns. His story was still in the early stages when, spurred by curiosity, his classmates asked him to share it with them. We felt it was time. Allen hesitated for the first couple of minutes. Embarrassed, he found it difficult to read. Finally he launched into an oral telling of his relationship to guns. His two brothers and the young adults in the neighborhood "needed a piece" for protection. His grandfather was a police officer who had a gun. People celebrated New Year's Eve by "shooting off guns." He paused again and asked for questions. Immediately, his progun narrative was challenged.

Paul summed up the questions. "Guns are dangerous. Will you put that in your story?" Allen's puzzled response was reflected in his eyes and posture. Until Paul asked this question, Allen hadn't really thought about it. "Maybe," he said.

The children's response to his ideas about guns was not lost on Allen. He took it as a compliment that they were interested. That night, Allen asked his grandmother about what the neighborhood had been like years ago. The next morning he announced in class what his grandmother had told him: Venders sold their wares up and down the streets. Families spent evenings talking on the front porch. Children played late into the evening on the sidewalks, front lawns, and partially blocked streets. The children's excitement was dampened when Allen explained that the streets aren't as safe anymore.

Over the next couple of weeks, a growing number of students stopped by Allen's desk to ask him about his story. He wrote feverishly, sensing its importance to others. Vicki wrote:

> I have noticed that Allen's views on guns have changed as he considers ideas for his writing. Originally he felt there were times when guns in homes were justified. He is more emphatic now that they are dangerous.

The process of writing helped Allen, but it also attuned him to the complexity of the issue. He heard arguments about gun abuse, yet he didn't want to write off the use of guns entirely. There was his grandfather, the policeman, who talked about guns and protection. There were his brothers and friends, who also talked about guns and protection. The issues tugged at Allen as he worked to fit them into a final written draft of "Guns." We were encouraged. When viewed as a process of continuing dialogue—with others and with himself—Allen's writing provided a context for reseeing and reaccessing the gun conflict. Over the month of April, Allen presented his revised story many times to small groups of friends. By May, as the children were selecting pieces for their upcoming published anthology,

Allen requested one last time to unveil his latest version. He hesitated only a moment before he began his almost flawless reading of the story he proudly held in his hands.

GUNS

Guns are nothing to fool around with. Parents should hide guns away from children. Children shouldn't play around with guns anyway. So I think guns is no good at all. Some people have guns in our neighborhood. We can do something about it. I will do my best and to try my best to stop the guns in my neighborhood. I will guarantee you it will stop. It will stop! I promise you.

It is time to use guns. When you are a police officer it is OK to use guns. Guns do kill people. Sometimes when some people are used to guns they are lucky and don't get hurt. Some police get shot when they are on duty. That is so-so-so sad when they get shot on purpose.

Why is guns bad for our children? Some people think guns are for safety. I think guns are for protection. Some people sell drugs to get guns. I think guns is just a piece of trash. But if it wasn't for weapons people wouldn't get killed. But some people ask for peace but so you think they get it when they use guns? What do you think about it?

We fondly recall Allen's final class reading of "Guns." The class was excited for him. It was almost as if the story Allen read belonged to all of us. But if Allen had included other children's ideas about guns, clearly the writing was singularly his. The story expressed his own conflict: some people can use guns and not get hurt. That seems to be OK to Allen. Yet if people, and significantly children, get hurt by guns, then guns are bad. The questions at the end suggest that an ongoing debate is necessary, and that such a debate might begin when others read Allen's story.

After submitting "Guns" to the student publishing committee that was preparing the class anthology, Allen reflected on the impact his story might have on others. He seemed to be calling on his grandfather (a police officer) for advice. "I want police officers to read it." For the most part, however, he was more interested in the reactions of other children. "It might help them, like, if their mothers have [pause] if their father have guns, the kids can sit around and talk to them like 'we shouldn't use it' because you shouldn't use it that way, and other stuff on it. They would probably read it and probably think—he's right! If I do keep on playing with guns I might get *killed,* and I don't want ta get k-killed. If they don't want ta die, and they messin' around with guns, they *must* want ta die. I just wanted ta change their minds."

Allen's writing gained him respect in the classroom. It also provided him with the opportunity to change in positive ways. We saw evidence of this change as the school year moved into the humid days of early June. His attendance improved dramatically. He was more willing to use his time in class constructively. He took an active role in publishing the class anthology. Yet at the time of Allen's greatest gains as a writer and thinker, we were nevertheless only cautiously optimistic about the lasting impact of Allen's story on his own life. We knew that writing, thinking, and debating about guns would not prevent him from experiencing the culture of guns in his own home and on the neighborhood streets. Over the summer break, we waited hopefully for Allen's return to school.

The following fall we received some disturbing news. Allen was in fifth grade and one of the oldest children attending the elementary school. As we watched him from across the hall, he looked out of place in a more traditional classroom. He worked alone at his desk whenever he showed up for class. Vicki discovered that Allen's custodial aunt had become sick in the late summer, and Allen had moved in with his grandmother. She lived several miles from the school, and transportation was often a problem. Vicki wondered how she could help. The publication of the anthology proved timely. Many of our students from the year before were members of Allen's fifth-grade class and we asked them all, including Allen, to a celebration of their publication. There would be book appearances and a time to renew community bonds.

On the day the book was distributed at school, Allen was noticeably absent. Later in the day, Vicki called his grandmother's home to inquire. Car trouble. Allen was infuriated that he had missed getting his copy of the book with the rest of the children. Vicki promised to drop one off after school. It was then that Vicki offered to drive Allen to school, all year if necessary, so he wouldn't miss any more classes. Allen's grandmother insisted that Allen could make it to school on most days, but she accepted Vicki's assistance temporarily. The next morning Vicki arrived at Allen's door at 7:15. No one answered her repeated knocks, and she drove off disappointed. But at 9:30, Allen raced up the stairs to Vicki's classroom. He had taken a bus. "Are you happy to see me?" he said. He spoke about his pride in the book, especially his story. In case anyone asked, he was happy to share his story with others.

Despite the pact between Vicki and Allen, his attendance was not consistent during most of the fall: he was moving back and forth between his aunt's and his grandmother's houses, depending on his aunt's health. Even Allen's involvement with his story waned. His grandmother told Vicki that kids in the neighborhood teased him because of the book. They thought it was silly. They wanted him to act as if school wasn't important. Allen's older brothers teased him as well. In late November, Vicki was alerted by some of her former students that "Allen was acting out in class." Once again, she looked for ways to entice him to use his passion for more constructive kinds of learning. With permission from Allen's fifth-grade teacher, Vicki began to "borrow" him for thirty to forty-five minutes a day. Her new writers could use the help of an experienced writer, and she hoped to resurrect some of the enthusiasm he had shown for writing the previous spring. Vicki's third and fourth graders were captivated by Allen's sense of the gun issue. On his visits from across the hall, he talked about stray bullets and about change. "We *can* do something about it," he repeated. We valued his visits.

We were also fortunate that at about that time, Allen, along with the other student authors whose writing was included in the anthology, was invited to present his story during a Martin Luther King celebration at a nearby university. For three weeks leading up to the Christmas break and two weeks afterwards, Allen prepared to perform his story and lead a discussion group of interested participants. He practiced on stage in the auditorium, his wide eyes peering over the podium that threatened to engulf him. He practiced in Vicki's classroom before school and during lunch. His story had become a badge of merit. His attendance and his attitude toward school improved.

After the celebration, however, Allen's interest in school waned again. His teacher confided to Vicki, "He is headed for trouble. He disrupts the class." Two days later, Allen was suspended from school—three days—for fighting. On the last day of his suspension, Vicki drove by his grandmother's home. He was playing basketball, a daily ritual since his suspension. When she offered to drive him to school the next day, he reluctantly agreed. She arrived early the next morning, but Allen was not waiting. She knocked on the door and drove around the block looking for him for twenty minutes. No Allen. Discouraged, Vicki drove to school by herself.

When she called the house, Allen said he didn't need a ride anymore. It was several days before he returned.

The morning of his return, he walked proudly down the hall with a small group of friends. Vicki made a point of meeting him in the corridor. Allen's admiring friends were jealously gathered around him. He was wearing a gift from his older brother, an oversized starter jacket with the team colors of a professional football team. A six-inch-high gun was silk-screened in blues and grays on the back of the jacket, its barrel framed by three-inch gold letters that read PRODUCT OF THE ENVIRON-MENT. Vicki was alarmed, but before she could respond, Allen turned to go into the classroom. As he moved away, her eye caught the gun on his jacket. The gun barrel and the oversized slogan appeared to engulf everything: the children, the locker-lined walls, the doors, and even the hallway itself. Before Allen disappeared behind the classroom door, Vicki refocused her gaze on him, and the nine-year-old child reappeared, a child who questioned his place in a culture that deified guns.

Allen was dismissed from school early that year. Despite Vicki's willingness to help him with after-school tutorials, invitations to cultural centers nearby, and rides to school, he gradually drifted away from the daily routine of attendance. Two weeks after he started wearing the starter jacket to school, Vicki wrote a hurried e-mail note to Dan.

> Allen was excluded today because he came to school with a starter gun. It has the look of a real pistol and I understand he was showing off and holding up kids in make-believe fashion on the playground. I don't know . . . The assistant principal insists he will go to court. I asked if there was any way to get him help. She laughed skeptically.

Several days later, Allen appeared on the playground after school. He hesitated when Vicki called to him. He didn't have much to say except to mention that he didn't know the length of his suspension. With only six weeks left in the school year, Vicki realized the urgency of the situation; after meeting with the assistant principal, she and his grandmother feared the worst. At the school's insistence, there would be court proceedings, but not until late spring. It was a slow process, one in which Allen was likely to be lost in the shuffle.

Four weeks later, Vicki again wrote to Dan.

> Allen is still out of school waiting for a court hearing. Apparently, the assistant principal has sent home some school work, but he may not

return to classes until there is a hearing. I called a friend at the Youth Home who said there is a possibility that Allen will not be allowed back in the school system next year. He may have to attend a private school or go to another district. Not good—an invitation to drop out of school.

As Vicki feared, Allen did not return to school that spring. He did not appear in court until mid-June.

◫◫◫

Dan reached for the January news article and read out the police chief's final comments: "The city will try to stop the custom of firing guns in the air to celebrate New Year's Eve." Vicki picked up a 1990 interview with Allen, and she and Dan read a highlighted section together:

We can celebrate with our families, and we can celebrate with our friends. We don't have to celebrate with gunfire.

◫◫◫

Note: In 1996 Allen has managed a comeback. As a sophomore in high school, he is poised to beat the odds, which state that only 30 percent of young black males who start high school finish. Allen's progress is evident in other areas of his life as well. In a recent conversation with Vicki, he expressed concern about a friend who dropped out of school the year before. "He carries a gun," Allen said. "I think he's headed for trouble."

We are not certain how Allen managed to beat the odds that defeat so many young men in his community. We would like to think that he has found it useful to engage in dialogue with others about issues that threaten to overwhelm him.

Anika: "Serious Talk" About Writing

A nika begins again and again. She writes a few lines on one page, then moves on to a clean page. She has a difficult time concentrating. There are too many distractions: the grinding of a pencil sharpener, two companions across the room whispering their secrets, the fight on the playground this morning, Danielle swearing in math class. One last time Anika returns to her writing, a word or two before the lavatory break when she is free once again.

A third grader, Anika was a reluctant writer. By the end of the year, her writing folder was full, but empty. Her stories rambled on over four to five pages yet they remained incomplete. Poems, with titles only, accounted for several other sheets of paper stuffed into her worn folder. There were two lengthy stories copied from a book. Her original ideas for writing a story or poem seemed frustrated. Anika's most complete work was a list, one that she polished and reworked for a couple of weeks, in between distractions. It appeared to be her favorite.

MY IDEAS PAPER

- write a story
- write a poem
- write a paragraph
- read a book
- Do something for others
- Make a thing like this ( )
- Circle all words you can't spell
- read ea word carefully
- Stop at the periods
- Indent P
- Conference

Anika was serious about her education. However, we were at our wits' end trying to understand her literacy learning. Nothing we did seemed to encourage her to write more thoughtfully. At the same time, she thrived in oral learning situations, assuming leadership roles at every turn.

The following year, Vicki requested that Anika be placed in her fourth-grade language arts class. We were eager to uncover some explanation for her lack of interest in writing. Perhaps it was her unusual shyness, which Vicki noted more than once in her journal.

Anika often arrives at school before the other children. She stands beside her locker awkwardly fumbling with her bulky purple hooded coat. I want to ask her if the coat is warm enough. She acts a bit self-conscious as I approach, looking down and hesitating before she speaks. She removes her hood and is unsuccessfully managing her hair which is sticking out in all directions. Embarrassed, she attempts to flatten it. Our eyes meet and we both turn our glances. The quietness of the building echoes the muffled shouts of the arriving children playing near the front entrance of the school.

We noticed that Anika kept to herself around adults. Perhaps the writing workshop, where teachers hovered about in close contact with student writers, intimidated her. Yet, looking more closely, we witnessed Anika's more aggressive side. In fact, sometimes she was downright pushy.

In early September, we observed a scene reminiscent of eight-year-old Anika, a young student leader who was gaining confidence with her skill. She suggested a plan for organizing and facilitating group discussions, an alternate means of sharing the students' writings from their reading Reflection Journals. Anika was frustrated with our monotonous form of one-at-a-time presentations and requested a moment to speak to the class.

> When one person talks at a time, we don't get to hear everybody. I think we should find another way, like I was saying before. Can we have a little group in the back of the room so that kids who want to read and get comments can? Then the people who want to read and don't want to talk don't have to.

In one brief moment, Anika had solved a problem that had bothered her and other children since we had initiated the shared readings. Shyness aside, she definitely was motivated to act, and with good ideas, when the desire moved her. Her classmates respected her and supported her creative suggestion.

In our search for reasons to explain why Anika hesitated to write, the strongest evidence suggests that she had difficulty with written language in a whole context. When there was a sustained time for writing she seldom stayed on task. Discomfort. We observed similar responses during concentrated reading periods. Why the uneasiness? Why the struggle?

On numerous occasions during Anika's first few weeks as a fourth grader, Vicki watched her as she tried to study.

> Anika rubs her forehead as she reads. She continually looks up in search of distractions. She dodges the sunlight as it focuses on her desk. Every once in a while she hides behind her book pretending to read. She flips the pages, too rapidly, yawning and raising her hands to stretch. Distracted by the sun in her eyes, she asks me, "Can I move?" I answer, "Yes."

> Anika moves closer to a group of friends and into the direct sunlight. At last, she seems to mirror the others' reading behaviors.

Anika's oral reading confirmed our prior observations. She read quickly, slurring her words and often misreading sections of sentences.

She interrupted her reading constantly to ask questions. Even so, her behavior did not answer our pressing question, "Why is Anika reluctant to write?"

Despite her seeming difficulty with reading and writing, Anika's results on tests assessing her language usage were adequate. She made sure Vicki didn't forget to dictate the required weekly spelling test. She even requested that we resurrect the basal reading texts we had unceremoniously retired to a back shelf. "I like those exercises," she explained, as if reading and writing made more sense to her when they were structured according to the basal series.

It was Albert Einstein who put Anika's uneven written work into perspective for us. In a letter, he wrote that for him, "Conventional words have to be sought at laboriously." He found it difficult to understand ideas through words, and thought more creatively through visual images. Perhaps Anika, too, was more visually oriented and did not yet see a place for language in her visual scheme. Certainly, she always seemed to grasp the big picture when we discussed issues in class. Her thinking was sharp, and she was especially good at untangling the ideas that collected in her mind.

We decided not to push Anika but to try to help her organize her thoughts. Late in the fall of her fourth-grade year, Anika demonstrated a new interest in reading. In an effort to impress her friends, who were reading more difficult books than she was, Anika challenged herself. She attempted one of Mildred Taylor's young adolescent novels. Now she paid less attention to distractions, and when it was time for a reading from a Reflection Journal, Anika's hand shot up. Holding her elbow for support, she waved her arm vigorously. She was determined to display her connection to the book *Roll of Thunder, Hear My Cry* and its author. "Mildred Taylor wants to tell about how blacks treat whites and whites treat blacks. I agree. I think this is my second book I read from her. She put meaning in it like it is happening right then. I think that's her career." As she spoke, Anika gestured with her hands, her elbows jutting out at her sides. She clasped her hands behind her head and continued, "I can tell what kind of person she is by her writing. The main thing of the story is that she is trying to be around people to stop people." By this time, some of the other children were confused and did not hesitate to interrupt. It was of little use. The more Anika explained, the more chaotic her answers got, yet all the while she was thriving in the self-created turmoil. Later we understood

Anika's point. Taylor wrote to attract an audience. If she could gain their attention perhaps she might convince them to condemn acts of prejudice.

We learned an important lesson from Anika's roundtable. Like Taylor, she needed an audience to discuss pressing issues. And as she strived to convince her audience of her opinions, she became more articulate. Looking more closely, we recognized something familiar in Anika's actions: she loved social situations where problems and people converged. It seemed to be inherent in her very nature. A further observation helped us frame this idea more clearly. Vicki wrote:

> Anika was in the corridor before the bell again today. Waiting. Her corner locker is positioned to view those approaching the second floor by three of the four building stairways. She is always the first upstairs and hesitates in that spot, usually fumbling with her backpack while she closely observes the clusters of children racing up the nearby stairs. They were reviewing new baseball cards and talking about the latest television special, rap, or outside fight. She waits patiently for her network of friends, anticipating the moment when she can share a nine-year-old's important concerns. As Anika's classmates gather she accesses the daily situation for each one. Their personal concerns are the subject of interest for her active mind. In rapid fire she speaks: "Janise isn't coming today and I betcha' a lot of kids are gonna stay home too. Yolanda was excluded because she picked a fight with Juanita. Did you hear what happened?"

The problem became one of channeling Anika's enthusiasm for solving social problems into opportunities for more productive writing. It proved to be a slow process. Anika's verbal prowess did little to convince her to write enthusiastically or creatively.

In the first part of her fourth-grade year, Anika's writing resembled the lists she had laboriously worked out in third grade. She often volunteered to be the recorder for a group or an all-class discussion. At times she made notes on the chalkboard while simultaneously orchestrating a lively class discussion. Anika also favored "lists" in her editorial comments on peer writing. In one case, she listed dos and don'ts as a result of a peer counseling session with two students who had been fighting. Anika later reminded one student that the list would be important in remembering what to do when they were challenged or had the urge to fight. We hoped that the success of Anika's masterminded project would encourage her to draw from her own listed comments in writing an essay or a story. However, as it turned out, she did not write about the topic again that year. Yet the occasion seemed to give her confidence as a thinker, and we viewed this as progress.

Eventually, Anika's confidence as a negotiator grew. One day she gathered the class together for some "serious talk." Something Mark had written, she thought, was cause for everyone's concern. His poem "Why Me" was a stark reminder of how children sometimes feel picked on and disliked. With her notes from the editorial committee in hand, Anika moved slowly toward the front of the room, motioning to her group to join her. Again she took charge, suggesting that Mark come to the front of the classroom to share his poem with the class. Mark nervously agreed.

"When I ask to help others they won't let me," Mark said in a disappointed voice. "Sometimes I'm happy on the inside but show sadness on the outside." He was solemn and teary eyed.

Off to one side, Ronald could barely contain himself and blurted out, "During art class I was threatened by you, Mark!"

Anika was ready. She had been waiting patiently for an opportunity to intervene. Reading from her notes and improvising on the spot, she addressed the question of why the students should be nice to Mark. "Mark, do you see where Ronald is talking about the same thing you are talking about in your story [poem]? You say people are saying mean things about you, but you may have made Ronald feel bad by the things you were saying about him. You can't do to Ronald what you don't want anybody to say about you."

Not much of an editorial comment, we thought. It was more like advice from a talk show host. This was not surprising, since Anika had enjoyed reading a short biography of Oprah Winfrey in our class library. Nevertheless, when Anika wrote down her thoughts for Mark, almost exactly what she had said in class, she showed some original thought and direction.

Halfway through the school year, Anika wrote her first fully developed story. Her writing was a response to Allen's story "Guns," which Anika had discovered in a student anthology in Vicki's classroom. For several days, Anika read selections from the book, until one day she exclaimed, "There are mistakes in this book! He [Allen] shouldn't say police should kill people! No one has a right to kill anyone."

Vicki sympathized with Anika. "Hmmm. This was Allen's message two years ago. Maybe he feels differently now. If you have something to say, you can talk or write to Allen."

The class discussion that day bloomed into one of those special moments teachers remember ever after. Students were interacting, thinking for themselves, teaching as well as learning, and overcoming the usual roadblocks to critical thinking. Anika was stimulated to write about her response to "Guns." And in what now appears to be an effort to keep the discussion alive, she wrote an editorial essay—not copied from a book and not a list of questions, but her own version of the event.

TODAY IN CLASS

Today in class we talked about "Guns." Allen wrote about guns. I think this is a pretty good story. But I think he had the wrong idea about guns. Allen said that guns was ok for police to kill people, with guns. But it is not ok for people who were not cops. I wish I could talk to Allen. I would tell him I didn't agree with what he said about guns! I don't think it is good to have guns especially around kids. Because kids need to grow up. I am not saying grown ups should die, but kids should grow up.

As an addendum to her essay, she wrote a letter to Dan, who was away from school that day.

Dear Dan, I have read Allen's story about guns. I did not like his story. I just didn't agree with what he said about guns . . . He said it was ok for police to shoot people and I don't agree with him. If I do see Allen I will help him with his story.

Dan wrote back.

Anika, sometimes writers need to consider the comments of editors and friends. I'm not sure Allen was asking for help, but I'm sure if he wants it your comments will help. Why don't you work to make some of your own writing better by being a responsible editor of your own writing? If you do as good a job with your own writing as you've done with Allen's, your writing will be great!

At the time, Dan thought his letter might just steer Anika into thinking more seriously about her own writing. Now we laugh at Dan's naiveté. Anika would have none of it. In her mind, her writing served the same purpose as her discursive encounters with her classmates: to keep stirring the pot, to rekindle the argument she had started until she was satisfied with the answer. If her writing did that, then certainly no revision was necessary. What motivated Anika to write was the social moment, and although the essays she wrote were indeed thoughtful and well crafted, they were secondary to Anika's real needs as a language user.

In her class journal, after an extremely cold February day when many children stayed home from school, Vicki wrote,

> Eight children came to school for the half day today. It was below zero outside, and the streets were heavily snow covered. Many districts in our area have cancelled classes several days this week. Not ours. Attendance in our school has been poor, but those who come to our class know that they will get extra attention from me. We have the leisure, with fewer children, to do our day differently.
>
> We met at the door with hugs, friendlier than usual, and quickly decided to read at the long table. The children felt so mature sitting tall on the stools. The sunlight they complain about at their desks went unnoticed as it shone above and between our new dinosaur curtains. It danced around the shadows of our bodies and books, adding a little extra warmth to out meeting place. A cozy squeeze. We bumped and brushed each other in order to fit, but it was comfortable. One child said dreamily, "I hope nobody else comes. If they do, we don't have room and they'll have to go to the discussion corner." I knew they were reveling in the comfort of a small group.
>
> Immediately I began to read, beginning the day with our same quiet ambiance. The room was silent, there were few distracting movements I glanced at Anika, who was sitting across from me. She looked around to see what everyone else was doing. Anika did not seem interested in the reading. She took some time to find the place in her book.
>
> The efforts of our group were concentrated and the quiet was conducive to study. Anika was the least interested in her reading, continually looking up to see what the others were doing. About thirty minutes later, as the others began to write in their Reflection Journals, Anika looked up at me and said, "I don't know what to write!"
>
> "Sure you do. Did you have feelings about the story? Tell how you feel."
>
> Anika nodded affirmatively. "I know what I'll write." Her tall body leaned over her book and she began. Now and then she looked up to

check what the others were doing. Finally resigned, she stayed on task for an extended period, commenting on her feelings in response to her reading.

In a small group discussion, Anika shared what she had written about Mildred Taylor and prejudice. She devoured the attention she received and made sure everyone understood where she stood. Then, as the others turned their attention to writing stories and poems, Anika moved in among them to work on her new story, one about the homeless. The narrative was remarkably similar to one Vicki had written and shared with the class a couple of days earlier. Two things became apparent to us. First, Anika's story, like her reflections on Taylor, was written while she was a participant in a select social gathering. It was important to her that she have a voice in the small group. And second, by writing about homelessness, as it later became apparent, Anika hoped to resurrect the vibrant discussion and social atmosphere that Vicki's earlier story had evoked. She wrote:

THANKSGIVING FOR HOMELESS

On Thanksgiving Day, I think people should have a place to stay and food to eat, but there are a lot of homeless people who don't have anything to eat or a place to stay and sleep. If I was grown, I would have a place for homeless people. People would stay, and if they had no food, I would give it to them. I saw a picture on t.v., and it was the day before Thanksgiving, and it was telling how people were trying to help homeless on the holidays. But why can't they do it everyday?

Sometimes I go to the store with my mom, and I see homeless people living in cardboard boxes and eating out of the trash. I think it's sad that people have to live like that. If I had the chance, I would do something about it. I am going to try to help the homeless right now by trying to save money for food and a home for them.

"Thanksgiving for Homeless," on a social issue, was a story from which Anika hoped to get a lot of mileage in further discussions, and in fact she did. The following year, when Anika returned to Vicki's classroom as a fifth-grade student teacher, she often drew on her Thanksgiving story to engage third-grade writers in conversations about writing. Yet, curiously, she never wrote any more about the subject. In fact, she wrote very little during her fifth-grade year.

Anika was convinced that writing was a way to engender conversation about issues and to stimulate others to write, but it did not convince her to write more herself. She could revise and assimilate ideas even if she didn't write. As teachers of language, we need to think seriously about Anika as we go about trying to find a place for writing in the education of our students.

Taria: The Power of Language

Vicki pressed her back against the chair and rested her elbows on the kitchen table. Slowly she settled her head in her hands in a gratifying exhaustion. The last couple of days had been significant, an unusual first week of teaching. As the evening light illuminated her journal page and reflected off her pen, she began to write.

It's beginning to come together quickly this year. I am determined to work on writing skills with the third graders as I have in the past with our fourth graders. Late Monday afternoon a new student, eight-year-old Taria, came to my classroom.

Her head was full of tiny braids with four small beads at the end of each. She was accompanied by her mom, three preschoolers, and a family friend. Taria comfortably interpreted, in sign language, the conversation between her deaf mom and me as I talked about our schedule and other details. I invited the family inside our classroom. I thought it was a great way to include our new student, Taria. I talked to the class about Taria's special skill—she signed using a different language to communicate with her hearing-impaired mom. Taria's alert eye movements made her appear as dependent on seeing as her mother is dependent on sign. I'm not sure my students understood.

In her first few conversations with Taria's family, Vicki learned that Taria had always been a precocious child, especially when it came to language fluency. At one year, she had already started to sign. Her mother said she would point to herself with her forefinger, then carefully shape Taria's tiny fingers until they represented the word *Mom*. Taria's verbal skills also flourished. By the age of five she was her mother's main interpreter. Grocery clerks, ministers, and neighbors depended on Taria to convey her mother's requests and inquiries. Confident and patient, Taria has become her mother's voice.

Language plays an important role in Taria's life. Like other multilingual children, she understands, at least intuitively, that languages differ in nuance and structure. From our earliest encounters with her, we wondered how the class might benefit from her knowledge and her ease in moving back and forth between speech and sign. We envisioned a win-win situation. She could make a significant contribution to our discussions about how we use language to communicate with others, and the students could help her overcome some of her shyness around children her own age. We even saw Taria's experience with sign language, along with standard English and dialects, as a way to introduce the idea of "varieties" of English. Our students, for example, loved Mildred Taylor's books about black family life. But they stubbornly resisted reading aloud the parts in dialect, and they seldom wrote if they couldn't do so in standard English. We understand their reluctance, but we also believe that children should learn to appreciate the rich complexity of language they will encounter throughout their lives, including dialects they hear at home. At the time, we assumed that Taria would jump at the chance to teach us all about the power of language.

Throughout September and most of October, Taria shied away from the limelight. A wisp of a child, she moved almost unseen amid the daily commotion in the classroom. Despite her language fluency in writing, she found it difficult to talk to the other children. She didn't feel accepted. She didn't know how to approach her classmates, and it seemed that she didn't want to. We understood her reluctance when we overheard several children making fun of her secondhand clothing and her "large lips." When *The Nutcracker* came to the city, Vicki had an idea. Once or twice a year she liked to invite a small group of children to attend a cultural event in the downtown area. This year, she would invite Taria. She hoped that attending the ballet might encourage Taria and the other students to get to know each other better. In a classroom of thirty-six children, some, especially newcomers, get little attention.

In various ways, *The Nutcracker* propelled us all forward in our thinking about Taria. The story she wrote a few weeks later describes that experience.

SIGN LANGUAGE AND NUTCRACKERS

My mom taught me sign language when I was a baby. I have a brother and a sister named Malcolm and Latoya. They know a little sign language, from the way me and my mother talk to each other. My mom always has been a good helper. She is hearing impaired and her name is Jackie. She was born with one blue eye and one black eye, but she can see very well. I love my mother more than you think.

One evening my teacher came to pick me up. I was surprised. She is a very nice teacher. We went to the Nutcracker Ballet and it was great. I learned how they made plays and dances. When they turned around it just made me want to do it too. It was at the Fox Theater. Outside it looked plain and flat, but inside it was a giant place. There were beautiful colorful things all around and there was gold in the ceiling.

At the Nutcracker Ballet I saw a deaf woman, and I asked my teacher did she want to go there and talk to that lady. In the middle [intermission] of the ballet we went to the lady and talked for a little while about my mother. The lady was there with her sister who can talk and sign like me and my mom. And then my teacher took me home.

For several days before the ballet, Taria sat at the back of the classroom studying a book about *The Nutcracker*. Even before she attended the event, she knew the music and excitedly described each dance and scene to Vicki. Once at the theater, her wide, dark eyes were alert to every detail—the acrobatic leaps, the planned chaos, the body language of arms, legs, heads, and torsos moving in synchronous motion to create a story. Intermission. And in the hallway of the grand theater, Taria readily signed with her "lady" friend, re-creating the story of the ballet and telling about their lives. Vicki watched Taria as closely as she did the stage. So did the other children. They saw Taria and her new friend speaking in sign. Taria was unfazed by their stares. For her this familiar situation was a comfort zone.

The next Monday, the children who attended the ballet led a class discussion. Six children's voices overlapped in telling various versions of the evening's events. Then, as if choreographed, the cacophony of voices stopped. During a momentary lull, one child began a story about Taria. "This lady and Taria were doing all these hand things, and they were so fast . . ." She described what she saw. The class was puzzled. One child made guttural sounds and told a friend that he'd heard deaf people speak that way. He mentioned Taria's mother.

Taria straightened up in her chair and shook her head. "No, my mom doesn't speak that way. My mom can be understood." The children deluged her with questions. "How come you can hear?" Taria seemed exasperated. She found it difficult to understand why her classmates questioned her own hearing just because she had deaf parents. Vicki intervened to move the discussion in a more positive direction.

"Taria," she asked, "would you sign for the class?"

Taria balked. Why was she the only one in the classroom responsible for knowing about the world of the hearing impaired? Her words silenced us. She was right. Apologetically, we acknowledged the awkwardness of the situation and went immediately to our trump card: "Recess."

Looking back, we realize that this experience could have caused a setback for Taria. But Taria has an inner strength that is obvious as soon as one gets to know her. And despite feeling hurt by some of the students' questions, Taria began to blossom. Her curiosity was piqued by our ignorance about the hearing impaired.

As anticipated, in time, Taria would teach us, but first, she needed to reflect and frame her ideas. It was during this reflective period that she found a book about Helen Keller and her teacher, Anne Sullivan. The more she read about them, the more they inspired her. Taria devoured the book. And in spite of our classroom policy, which encourages children to put their books back on the shelf at the end of the day, the book more or less became Taria's. She wrote in her journal:

I could be obnoxious about the book and make people not like it, and I would keep it for a very long time.

We responded enthusiastically and quickly. "You can keep it in your desk Taria, but if other children want to read it you must share." She didn't have to worry; the book was not a favorite in our class, and it was hers to hoard if she wanted.

In her journal, Taria wrote,

Helen was a blind girl and she was deaf. I have a father and a mother who are deaf. I know how people feel when they are deaf. I feel sorry for people like that. I love this book very much. I really appreciate for this book to be written by a blind and deaf person. Mrs. Sullivan was a helping, lovely teacher. Her and Helen made a game about language, how to help Helen learn and do language. Annie was almost blind and her eye broke out, but she still helped Helen. I wish Helen was alive today so I can talk to her and tell her about my mother. When I was writing my journal about Helen I realized that I feel good for her and my mother. Hearing impaired people can learn fast. My mother is smart and she tries to control in talking to someone. She is a fast learner. Helen did lots of words with Mrs. Sullivan's hands. Mrs. Sullivan put her hands in Helen's hands and told poems and stories. Helen is a woman that could survive.

Later, at the end of one of her final journal entries about Helen Keller (and while involved in a first draft of her story "The Nutcracker Ballet"), Taria printed, in large letters, SIGN LANGUAGE TODAY PLEASE! Helen Keller and Anne Sullivan taught Taria to trust her own beliefs about the significance of sign and to appreciate her gifts as a language user and an interpreter for the hearing impaired. Eventually, Taria did teach others, but not in the way we had first imagined and not until she was able to trust her peers and her teachers. It was interesting to us that Taria, like Helen Keller and Anne Sullivan, made connections between trust, language, and life. As Taria showed us, meaningful living is always contingent on communication and trust.

For two weeks during the school year, Taria attended school while suffering from an abscessed tooth. At first, Vicki noticed what seemed to be Taria's reluctance to talk. But later in the week, she observed Taria's discomfort when the child winced several times during the morning. Vicki intervened and set up an appointment for Taria with a reliable dental clinic.

"Don't worry, Taria, they are a good team of dentists that specialize in caring for children."

"Will it hurt?"

Vicki comforted her. "No, I don't think so."

At 8:00 A.M. Taria entered the dentist's office for the "painless" treatment. By 11:00 A.M., she was back in class. Silent and brooding, she went about her work. That evening Taria called Vicki at home. Vicki held her breath for a moment before she spoke.

"Hi Taria, I was surprised to see you at school this afternoon. Did you have to take any medicine?"

Taria's voice had a slight edge. "My mother does not want me to miss school so she brought me there from the dentist. But Mrs. Rybicki, don't you understand that you told me that it wouldn't hurt?" The story of her emotional ordeal poured out.

"Taria, what I meant was that they would be able to fix your tooth better than they did at that other clinic. This time it will heal. Rinsing with Listerine and brushing your teeth is not going to heal the sore in your mouth."

"Oooh, but Mrs. Rybicki, I can't forget that you told me it won't hurt. Mrs. Rybicki, I am going to write a story today and you will see how it was. They tricked me, and you tricked me too."

Vicki apologized, but Taria was silent. As she hung up the phone, Vicki felt empty. She had let Taria down, and just when this gifted child was starting to open up . . . Her thoughts turned to Taria's story. *How will the other children react? Will they lose faith in me too?* We would soon find out. Two days later, Taria presented her story to the class. It was a remarkable first draft, conceived in passion and pain, and little different from this final version:

MY DENTIST APPOINTMENT

Last week my teacher, Mrs. Rybicki, was mad with my dentist because the dentist did not take care of my teeth right and my abscess was still hurting. My teacher made another dentist appointment for my abscess. She said my teeth would not hurt at all when I went to this dentist. I believed my teacher for that.

The next day I went to the dentist. I was telling my mother everything my teacher had said to tell my mother. The dentist introduced himself and asked me a lot of questions. Dr. Peter told me to follow him, and I was laughing because I knew I was brave.

Then I sat in the dentist chair for a few minutes. I felt comfortable there. They took an x-ray of my tooth. It did not hurt at all. The dentist told me to sit down on the couch and wait until he came back. This woman said, "Come here. I don't know why anyone left you out here by yourself."

Then, this man said he would numb me. Dr. Peter told me he was not going to pull out anything until he tell me what was going to happen. Everyone was around me like they had been another little girl I saw. She was crying, but I was brave because I knew my teacher had said it wouldn't hurt.

My mother came and left. She did not want to see me if I got hurt. So they shot me in my mouth with a needle and told me that they were going to put tubes in my mouth. I had two tears falling out my beautiful eyes. They had put jelly in my teeth and gums. I was so mad with my teacher when the dentist shot me, and when my dentist was finished with me, I got really mad at a lot of people.

After that I was still laying down on the chair and this man said, "Oh, there's my pumpkin pie. I didn't see you."

I said something in my mind, "You better get out of my face and pumpkin my foot."

Then a woman said, "Are you OK my dear?" I didn't say anything to her, but I said in my mind, "Leave me alone, I'm already mad with my teacher." Then I blurted out. "Oh, wait 'til I see Mrs. Rybicki. She told a big story to me about this." After that every time I saw Dr. Peter the same thing went through my mind.

Then I punched my hands and said, "I'm so mad at you, Mrs. Rybicki." I was so mad, so this man gave me a pencil, stickers, and balloons.

Then this other man put this cotton in my mouth and said, "I hope you get well." I said, "You better well my tooth."

When I came out of the dentist office I met my grandmother's friend. She had worked at Receiving Hospital a long time ago with my grandmother Sherri.

This dental emergency was a bad day for me but when I went back to school, the day was OK for me. Mrs. Rybicki said I would be alright. Because it was Valentine's Day, my mom said, "Taria doesn't need any candy from anybody."

When I got to school everybody was in the auditorium singing, "We Shall Overcome Someday." I couldn't talk at all. Everybody like Sarah Miles and Shaleena Masters was like, "What happened to you?" I tried to explain with my mouth hurting, but my teeth were sleepy from when I went to the dentist. Then everyone was singing again. It was only the 5th and 4th graders that were performing.

So everyone went to get pizza in the lunchroom. Elijah had to wait for a long time. We had three pieces of pizza each. Our juice tasted just like water to me. All my classmates were joking about the juice. Mrs. Rybicki was looking at me like I was crazy. Then she started laughing right along with me.

After that we went to our classroom to change Valentine cards. It was fun to me. I had a bad day today and then when I went to school I had fun. It was amazing what happened. "I had a good lucky day today," I said to myself.

Throughout Taria's reading, the room was buzzing. Serious faces let out squeaks of laughter in response to the words "You better well my tooth!" We looked at one another as the children peppered Taria with questions, and then we burst out laughing. The sense of trust had not been broken, it had just been bent a little. In fact, Taria's experience at the dentist, and her story about it, seemed to reinforce a growing sense of community and trust and motivate her to do some of her best work. Taria's story showed the other children how to use humor in writing to express feelings of fear.

Taria is like many of the children in this book: the more she trusts, the more she opens up. The more trust she inspires, the more those she touches also grow as human beings. In Taria's writing and conversations, the relationship between true communication and trust was a frequent theme. In "My Grandmother," a story about her eighty-four-year-old grandmother, for example, she wrote,

I wrote this story because my grandmother was really sad and almost had a heart attack about it. Her house burned down. She was getting ready to go home and I told her not to go home. I didn't want to break her heart by saying something . . . And then I just had to tell her about it and she just sat down and started crying. They were afraid to tell her. I asked my auntie and mother to tell her, but they thought it was too scary. You know, my grandmother's skin is all wrinkled, and you can tell she's a good person. By looking at you she looks at you like a hundred. She just looks at you real nice and says, "What did you say?" I couldn't stand it. I just closed my eyes and said it. I didn't tell her the people stole her stuff first, then burned her house down. It made me feel sad and uncomfortable. And then I get better by telling someone.

Taria's grandmother relied on Taria to tell her the truth. For her grandmother, Taria's story confirmed conversations about her house that she had overheard but refused to accept. She turned to Taria for the comfort of the truth. And by breaking the unhappy news to her grandmother and then writing a story to read to the class, Taria also felt better.

It has often been said that what makes human beings unique is language. We would add that it is the human capacity to communicate in multiple languages (how) for multiple purposes (why) that makes us truly remarkable. When we first met Taria, we marveled at the fluent gestures of her hands, eyes, and mouth as she signed to her mother. Within weeks we were listening attentively as she articulated her ideas. We absorbed the intricate stories she painstakingly wrote and seasoned with her personality. And we saw the crucial importance of the relationship between trust and language.

We realize that difficult issues can arise as trust becomes a factor in the language arts classroom. But by recognizing a child's need to use language critically, we encourage children to write in less "canned" ways and to tell more complex stories about their lives. That could be frightening for those who don't want to become involved, or who believe that they wouldn't know how to respond to the realities of some of these children's lives, and this is certainly something to consider. But for us, the danger of minimizing the importance of children's lives and their reasons for using language poses a much larger risk. Vicki's classroom is an extended community resource for the neighborhood where our students live. John Dewey, a prominent figure in education, once wrote that "What the best and wisest parent wants for his own child, the community wants for all its children." The parents and guardians of the children we teach have asked us to honor the reality of the children's lives. During regular parent conferences, Vicki often asks the visiting care-givers what they think of the children's stories, essays, and poems they see displayed in a large magazine format at the back of the room. Invariably, they respond, "The children are telling it like they see it." With this in mind, we constantly ask ourselves: How can we *not* listen to the life stories that children want to share? We trust that our students' stories will change those who read them.

While writing about Taria, we paused to question the effect of her sense of language on her classmates. They did not always seem to notice her remarkable ability to understand language and shape and reshape it for specific purposes. Her insights may take some children longer to absorb, but we like to think that Taria has left a lasting impression. And we hope that, in the long run, they will see as vividly as she does how truly amazing the power of language can be.

Conclusion

We conclude this book with interviews for two reasons. First, we want to clarify some of the underlying questions readers might have about our work, such as how Vicki, who has lived and taught in the same community for thirty-one years, approaches pedagogical and philosophical decisions. We believe that if we had attempted to focus too much on our own commentary earlier, we might have drawn attention away from the children's lives as literacy learners. Second, as we have worked together over the past five years we have come to understand the value of the interview as dialogue and its narrative structure as a way of learning from one another. What follows is a synthesis of some of the typical questions we asked ourselves during our collaboration. These questions have stimulated our own thinking, time and again, in constructive and unexpected ways.

🔲🔲🔲

DAN: *Does the teacher have a responsibility beyond helping the child "feel better" through writing? For example, what are the intellectual, social, and cultural imperatives of writing?*

VICKI: Because I am interested in the child as a whole person, I think that students' "feeling better" about themselves is an introductory step, an avenue to the intellectual. Writing in our classroom is relational, as is knowledge. The children begin to realize that writing is a way of knowing and expressing themselves and a way of knowing their world. I often find that when students feel better about themselves, they are more willing to share their ideas. Once they are able to share, questions about clarity arise. Their peers ask, "What do you mean by that?" The students then realize that they need to be clearer, and when they write, they struggle to make sense of their concerns and their ideas. Their revisions, with relevant detail and description, allow others to understand what they are trying to say.

As teachers we constantly ask ourselves how students' writing affects them and how it is affecting others. Our community process writing has become an instrument of change. The students' writing about themselves leads to learning in many different ways. For example, one student, Paul, had difficulty with his reading and writing skills in the classroom. Paul, however, was convinced of the importance of sharing his ideas. As he became more comfortable with his sharing, the social aspect of our Writers' Community, he became more in touch with the history of his culture. Paul related the violence in today's community with the slavery of African Americans in the past. His writing described the need for a belief in family commitment today. Paul's ideas led to further discussion. Along with other students, he conferred with a historian, and the children concluded their study by posting their published works on the walls of the classroom.

DAN: *What are some of your conclusions about Paul's work and his classmates' response?*

VICKI: The relational activity of sharing ideas and writing resulted in Paul's writing more. Knowledge was constructed among the others in the class, and they too became more involved in writing. The children begin to realize that writing is at once a way of knowing themselves and a way of knowing their world.

The students are enriched by their communication with an audience broader than the classroom. They better understand the need to comply with a more universal code of writing and speaking. They value their culture, their city, and themselves as young authors—repeated messages in their writings. The children believe that writing can change lives. It has helped them to value school-based literacy. The relational learning through writing, negotiating, collaborating, and knowing others has been an enabler for them.

DAN: *Is it necessary to create an atmosphere of trust in the classroom? If so, how do you create an atmosphere of trust with your students?*

VICKI: A basic characteristic of trust is honesty. As teachers, we cannot have a relationship in the classroom without trust. Gaining trust, however, involves risk. When I admitted to my students that I was not a writer, they were more willing to be honest with each other. They noticed that you and other adult visitors freely shared your writing. I soon found it necessary to explain that writing was difficult for me. I told them that I struggled with ideas and clarity when I wrote. They helped me by using the methods I had suggested to them. They asked me to list the topics that were of interest to me, and they promised to help me revise and edit my work the way they did each other's.

The students' trust in each other has been demonstrated repeatedly in their student editorial committees. One editorial group, which met to discuss Micah's poem, realized that the more important issue was Micah's relationships with his classmates. They asked Micah if the class might talk with him first. As Micah described the continued strain between him and his classmates, they spoke of his antagonistic ways toward them. The students' conversation and resolution to support each other exemplified sincere trust. And the open class negotiations led to a better understanding of Micah—and his poetry.

In order to gain trust, I must trust the students, and they each other. Each day we practice and model ways for all of us to help each other. I often arrange time for the students to meet on their own in less supervised situations. Small groups meet in an extra space under the stairs, in the corridor, or some other space. They decide on a specific task and assume responsibility for each other. I find that these situations allow the students to "take ownership" of their learning.

DAN: *Vicki, you have said that writing is something more than just a product—you see writing as a* tool *through which students gain insight into their lives. Can you explain this better?*

VICKI: When the students are given the opportunity to write what is important to them, they often write very personal thoughts. I suggest that they keep this writing "private." However, in time, many choose to share their "problems." They say that these problems have kept them from studying well. They also indicate that their problems directly interfere with their work as a writer. They have difficulty keeping focused on topics that are not directly related to their lives. Writing is indeed a personal matter.

Often, after the students have had an opportunity to share their difficulties, they desire to explore another genre, such as poetry, to express themselves. They believe that writing "gets their problem out" and that they are better able to cope. For example, one child who longed to have her mom back home wrote a story about her sadness at her mom's absence. Another child spoke about her mom being incarcerated, but she was asked by family members not to discuss the circumstances, which were heart-wrenching for her. Our class discussions and personal writing about our experiences with special "moms" led to poems about the aunts that were now care-givers for both of these students. Thus, they satisfied their social and psychological need to share an experience while also using language as a powerful expressive medium.

DAN: *If this were a more perfect world, but not necessarily a paradise, what would you like to see us be able to provide in schools to support learners better?*

VICKI: My typical enrollment has been thirty-five to thirty-seven students, a full classroom, without a teacher's aide. It would be ideal to have a smaller class size, but then again, a class of fifteen borders on paradise. I long for school staffs to recognize and respect the gifts of children (and each other), even when those gifts are expressed through different kinds of intelligence. We need to focus more energy on supporting students and building on their strengths, to catch glimpses of the positive and concentrate on what they know, to make learning exciting.

Faculties long for meaningful staff meetings, for landscapes where teachers and administration can support each other and work collaboratively. We need the times, places, and forums to share our own personal stories and our classroom stories.

I suggest that we create "revolving doors" for our classrooms. From the very beginning of the year, our classroom is a welcoming place. When parents come to introduce themselves and their children, I invite them in to introduce themselves to the class. We begin with a general invitation to share in our classroom experiences. I personally introduce myself on that first day and invite my husband during the first week of school for a storytelling session.

I provide opportunities for many different people to visit and share their expertise with the class.

Teachers need assistance with repetitive paperwork so that the classroom learning environment isn't constantly interrupted. I have found the relationship with classroom visitors—parents, former students (young authors who act as guest-teachers), preservice teachers, and members of the community—to be invaluable.

DAN: *What is the biggest problem your students face as inexperienced writers?*

VICKI: The students find my suggestion that they can become writers incredible. They ask, "How can I be a writer if I can't read, I can't spell, and I don't know grammar?" In most of their formal schooling they have studied language skills in isolation but have had little opportunity to practice them in an integrated way. Again, I ask for the students' trust. They will become writers, but their freedom of expression is first. When they share their writing, and the listening audience asks for clarity, students discover that it is necessary to standardize form so the reader understands the message. The writing process approach reverses the basal instructional program practiced in most classrooms. Teachers are often afraid of the individual nature of writing and the time needed to correct it. They have difficulty balancing the multiple conversations in a collaborative classroom.

DAN: *How has the development of this Writers' Community helped to mitigate students' fears about being writers?*

VICKI: I have found that the students develop control of their own learning through their writing. They talk about writing and reading not as an exercise but as an experience to which they relate. They interact with others through writing and express pride in being young authors. Amazingly, the students view writing as an adult exercise; they assume that all adults write. The students question visitors to the classroom about their uses of writing and certainly expect their teachers to be writers.

DAN: *It becomes obvious that not every teacher has the kinds of experience necessary for doing what you do in your classroom. How has your background prepared you to teach in the community to which you have dedicated most of your life?*

VICKI: My many years of experience in an African American neighborhood as a religious sister dedicated to community service certainly has been an asset to my developing practice as a teacher with folks of a culture other than my own.

On the other hand, we all have to begin somewhere. My personal background hasn't matched where I teach. My experience as a learner has been invaluable for me. I studied African American history at the university and repeatedly asked questions of the parents of my students. I asked parents to participate as storytellers and as readers of their own poetry and published words, especially those written in dialect and describing African American cultural traditions. Many responded to the invitation to share customs and culture for classroom celebrations, even in the 1960s, before it was in vogue.

Today, we need to look further. Our classrooms must venture beyond the walls of the school building. I have found it important to accept invitations for the students to present their writing to other communities, such as the two university-sponsored events you arranged, where our students shared their classroom-published writing on panels and opened discussions with preservice teachers and graduate students.

DAN: *How have you changed as a result of our collaboration?*

VICKI: When you first came to my classroom I was terrified. After all, I had returned to the university because I did not believe that I had that much to offer. Parents and teachers spoke highly of my work but few spent time with my students and me in our classroom.

From the beginning, you trusted my work. You continually affirmed me. There was always an excitement and interest in my classroom and our stories. You were unusual as a university colleague; the students always came first. As a researcher, you agreed with me that the students, as well as the research community, must benefit from your explorations. You introduced wonderful children's literature that respected the lives of many cultures and inspired relational learning for the students. We enjoyed talking about the stories and personally reflecting on their relevance to our own lives.

I appreciated your active engagement—talking to each child, sharing reading and writing with them. From this modeling, I became more free to be one of the readers and writers myself. I became a participant in my elementary classroom.

Your next step, Dan, was to tell others about our work. We began to open our classroom to preservice teachers, parents, former students, and members of the community. I now realize that I *need* "others" to share their stories and to support each of us as writers and readers, especially because of the confined structure of our schools and classrooms.

The collaboration with you through our conversations, your regular classroom visits, and our daily e-mail letters helped to raise my consciousness of classroom stories. It encouraged me to write them, to become aware of their importance, to value them. Your daily responses gave helpful suggestions and ideas for our young writers. Your interest and enthusiasm with the students and with me created the "inside-of-an-outside" audience. Through our collaboration, I viewed myself as a learner in the classroom.

Your trust in me and the students, together with the collaborative pedagogy supported in our classroom, has provided the students with important connections between school-based learning and their life world.

DAN: *In this book "we" represents our collaborative effort. I don't think we would be able to use this symbolic form of expression without your ideas about how you have come to incorporate the word "we" in the community of the classroom. Can you explain what you mean by "we"?*

VICKI: "We" represents the ownership of all those who participate in the teaching and learning experience. The classroom was never "my" classroom and the children never "my" students because there is always so much for us to learn from each other.

Naming the classroom "ours" assigned responsibility to the students. It is their space and they have wonderful ideas to share. The students know each other well and must assume some accountability for each other's learning and discipline. We aimed to work together and discussed decisions, such as welcoming others as participants in our educational experience.

For many years, Dan, you interacted with us as a regular participant. As your visits became less frequent, you continued to communicate with me through e-mail letters and with individual students. You suggested our classroom to many caring university students, who were generous with their time in our classroom. They studied with us, wrote with us, and shared their ideas. They too modeled the kinds of education and behavior that were being generated in our classroom.

The participation of two preservice teachers serves as a good example. Tegan created a more intense peer-teaching program. Sylvia's skill in complementing our writing program with music was powerful. Other educators and parents who volunteered their time to our class introduced literature through storytelling and the arts. Most who participated were interested in extending themselves personally to support the students' learning, even outside of class time. A few outside participants committed themselves even after school hours and continued to return long after their independent university study. I believe this happened because of the emphasis on the relational nature of our classroom.

回回回

VICKI: *On the first day you arrived at Franklin Elementary School you were asked two complex questions by the principal and the children in my fourth-grade class. Would you comment?*

DAN: The answers to both of those questions are similar. When the principal asked why I and my colleague Bill had come to Franklin, I said that, as a rural teacher for fourteen years, I too was aware of situations in which researchers came to my high school and appeared to be benefiting much more than the students or teachers. However, I learned firsthand about the possibility of a good collaboration with someone from outside the school. I told him of a university graduate student who came to my high school language arts classroom not only to learn but so that we could learn from one another. I said that was what I wanted to do in your classroom. I had a teaching agenda in which I would learn as much from the students and you as they might from my experience with literacy workshops. And I meant it.

Now, when your students got hold of me ten minutes later, their questions were similar but with a different twist. After you introduced me as a guest teacher who would be working in the classroom once or twice a week for the year, one student asked, "You are white, why would you want to come and work with us? Not very many people want to work with black children." The question caught me off guard. I had thought about that issue for a long time but had never come up with any definitive answer. Fortunately, your students were patient, which gave me time to respond as truthfully as I could. I told him that it was an opportunity to learn more about teaching eight- and nine-year-old children, something I had done only sparingly before. And I said I was there to learn as much as I could from him about him and about his culture because I could use my experience to grow as a teacher and person. He liked the idea that he could teach me, and I felt that he and the other students realized that their teaching had already begun.

From both experiences that day, I began to understand what you had been telling me in our graduate class about the meaning of teaching and learning within a community.

VICKI: *When I first invited you to the classroom, I was really hoping that you would be able to come once or twice a week for a year so that we could learn from one another. But as it turned out you stayed much longer than I expected—the next year,* *the year after, and often until just recently. How did we manage to fit into your more long-term agenda as a teacher and researcher?*

DAN: I came back for the same reason many other guests return to your classroom time after time. I have never stopped learning from my experiences in your classroom. One, even two years was not enough. But there is another reason, one I've shared with you before. We have both experienced collaborative situations in which a key player in the collaboration bails out after a short time. I didn't want to bail out on you or your students after I have made a commitment to our collaborative effort. I've felt the sting myself before. Besides, my students at the university would have been angry with me if I stopped coming. They loved to visit your classroom and saw a connection that was invaluable to them as preservice teachers. I guess we all got caught up in the learning situation that occurred as a result of our collaboration. I've never regretted my decisions.

VICKI: *Your answer leads me to another question. How have you changed as a result of your experience at Franklin and your experience in the community in which these students live?*

DAN: I have begun to understand better that change is integral to my pedagogy and my growth as a teacher. I have also changed in my perception of children as learners. In your classroom, I saw a reciprocal relationship between teaching and learning: students taught each other and learned from one another about friendship, hate, death, love, and what it was like to live in their community. They taught me how to be tolerant and how to write. They taught me that if you give children time and guidance they will write provocative pieces. Their writing process is similar in many ways to my own struggle as a writer. Words and ideas don't often flow easily. When we write there are so many starts and stops. I've learned from this experience of watching and working with students that we as teachers and parents need to give children space. They will succeed if we give them the same space and the same opportunities as writers that we ourselves need as teachers and adults: an inviting writing environment where our first attempts do not need to be our best and where we learn as much from feedback as from thinking about our own ideas. Children need to have a hand in shaping the writing environment at school and at home. They need to be able to decide what they write about as well as how they will share what they have written. By incorporating this kind of approach to children and writing in our writing curriculums, we will strengthen students' language skills.

And of course, I have begun to understand that children use many forms of expression—art, music, body language—as a way of knowing. It is "not knowing" that produces the kind of change we don't want as human beings, and which is deleterious to our growth, that of our children, and that of the communities in which we live.

VICKI: *How do you feel about our use of the word "we" in this book to describe our collaboration as writers and as teachers?*

DAN: I don't think we would have been able to use "we" as a symbolic form of expression if you hadn't described how you have come to incorporate the word "we" in the classroom. The first day I walked into your classroom, you talked about "we" as teachers, and "we" as learners. I've never forgotten that. "We" means those who work together to construct and shape a learning environment. "We" means the interdependence of all the people and institutions in a community in educating a child. Considering this interpretation, which I know you have also espoused, it was not a big leap to using the word "we" in our book, although here it mostly represents you and me, and it is the pronoun we use most often in narrating events and describing people.

I know that when we first started writing this book we couldn't agree on a perspective. We asked ourselves, Should one chapter come from your perspective, one chapter from a student's perspective, and so on? But finally we settled on a first-person perspective as the dominant one because it was consistent with our attempt to reinforce a way of thinking about teaching and learning that stresses community interdependence.

VICKI: *What do you think students have learned from our collaborative efforts to establish this Writers' and Readers' Community in my classroom?*

DAN: Well, your students have already published two anthologies of their poems, stories, and essays, plus a magazine that is posted weekly on the classroom walls. But of course quantity is not the only yardstick that measures success as a writer. Their skills have also improved, in that they are much more fluent writers than they were before they experienced the Writers' and Readers' Community. The biggest thing is that they have learned to learn from one another. They have learned to see literacy learning as a community effort. For example, to make their writing clearer, students seek out an editing group, which often influences them on issues of style and rules of grammar. This kind of learning is important for all children, but with a class like yours, of thirty-seven children, this kind of learning seems particularly important.

I have also learned that trust plays an important role in students' lives. When a student writes something he or she feels is important, that student writer needs to know that although others may disagree, they will not criticize or make fun of a piece of writing, that peers will offer useful comments. Students have to trust that their teacher will listen to their ideas and suggest useful avenues for presenting and clarifying them. Your students believe that reading and writing have a purpose beyond earning a letter grade—that reading and writing can produce change in their lives and the lives of others. This is good.

On a similar note, I have learned to see different kinds of student writing as purposeful. It has taken me a while to learn that not all student writing *should* look alike. Whatever children choose to write about, they think it is important. So, all of their writing matters to me. I have learned to look more closely at a piece of writing, no matter how long, to try to understand its significance to the writer. From that point on, I can work with the student in other areas, such as skills and style.

References

Alejandro, Ann. "Like Happy Dreams—Interpreting Visual Arts, Writing and Reading." *Language Arts*, 71, 1, pp. 12–21.

Ashton-Warner, Sylvia. 1963. *Teacher*. New York: Simon & Schuster.

Bunting, Eve. 1990. *The Wednesday Surprise*. Illus. Donald Carrick. New York: Clarion.

Calkins, Lucy, with Shelley Harwayne. 1991. *Living Between the Lines: The Art of Teaching Writing*. Portsmouth, NH: Heinemann.

Choi, SookNyul. 1993. *Halmoni and the Picnic*. Boston: Houghton Mifflin.

Clifton, Lucille. 1992. *The Lucky Stone*. Magnolia, MA: Peter Smith.

Dyson, Ann Haas. 1988. "Appreciate the Drawing and Dictating of Young Children." *Young Children*, 43, 3, pp. 25–32.

Graves, Donald. 1983. *Writing: Teachers and Children at Work*. Portsmouth, NH: Heinemann.

———. 1989. *Investigate Nonfiction*. Portsmouth, NH: Heinemann.

Greenfield, Eloise. 1991. "Buddy's Dream." In *Night on Neighborhood Street*. New York: Dial.

Hansen, Jane. 1987. *When Writers Read.* Portsmouth, NH: Heinemann.

Hubbard, Ruth. 1989. *Authors of Pictures, Draughtsmen of Words.* Portsmouth, NH: Heinemann.

———. 1990. "There's More Than Black and White in Literacy's Palette: Children's Use of Color." *Language Arts,* 67, pp. 492–500.

———. 1995. *A Workshop of the Possible.* York, ME: Stenhouse.

Johnson, Angela. 1993. *When I Am Old with You.* Illus. David Soman. New York: Orchard.

Little, Lessie Jones. 1988. *The Children of Long Ago: Poems.* Illus. Jan Spivey Gilchrist. New York: Philomel.

Maruki, Toshi. 1982. *Hiroshima No Pika.* Illus. Toshi Maruki. New York: Lothrop.

Mathis, Sharon Bell. 1986. *The Hundred Penny Box.* Illus. Leo D. Dillon and Diane Dillon. New York: Puffin.

Moline, Steve. 1995. *I See What You Mean: Children at Work with Visual Information.* York, ME: Stenhouse.

Murray, Donald. 1985. *A Writer Teaches Writing.* Boston: Houghton Mifflin.

Pascal, Francine. 1992. *Sweet Valley Kids: Elizabeth Meets Her Hero.* New York: Bantam.

Rosen, Harold. 1985. "The Nurture of Narrative." In *Stories and Meanings.* Sheffield, UK: National Association for the Teaching of English.

Spinelli, Jerry. 1992. *Maniac Magee.* New York: HarperCollins.

Tate, Eleanor E. 1994. *The Front Porch Stories: At the One Room School.* New York: Dell.

Taylor, Mildred D. 1991. *Roll of Thunder, Hear My Cry.* New York: Puffin.

Yolen, Jane. 1994. *Grandad Bill's Song.* Illus. Melissa B. Mathis. New York: Putnam.